# DEMENTIA

*a practical guide to Alzheimer's Disease and related illnesses*

# DEMENTIA

*a practical guide to Alzheimer's Disease and related illnesses*



LEONARD L. HESTON, M.D.
*Director of Adult Psychiatry*
*University of Minnesota*

JUNE A. WHITE
*Associate Scientist*
*University of Minnesota*

W.H. FREEMAN AND COMPANY
New York

Library of Congress Cataloging in Publication Data

Heston, Leonard L.
Dementia: a practical guide to Alzheimer's disease and related illnesses.

(A Series of books in psychology)
Includes index.
1. Presenile dementia. 2. Alzheimer's disease.
3. Senile dementia. I. White, June A. II. Title.
III. Series. [DNLM: 1. Dementia, Presenile. WM 220
H588d]
RC522.H47 1983 616.89'83 83-9018
ISBN 0-7167-1568-6
ISBN 0-7167-1569-4 (pbk.)



2 3 4 5 6 7 8 9 MP 1 0 8 9 8 7 6 5 3

Dedicated to Eva Pappas,
a victim, in whose memory her daughter,
Tess Galati, provided professional editorial advice.

A SERIES OF BOOKS IN PSYCHOLOGY

*Editors:*
*Richard C. Atkinson*
*Gardner Lindzey*
*Richard F. Thompson*

# CONTENTS

# INTRODUCTION

This book is about a group of diseases which affect the brain. They begin in middle to late-adult life, and some 30 percent of us will develop one or another of them if we live long enough. These illnesses are widely misunderstood, even by professionals. Because the results are much the same no matter which disease produces them, all are classed together in medicine as *dementias* or *dementing illnesses.* Alzheimer's disease is the best known of the group.

What they all produce is a steady inexorable decline in the function of the brain until death comes, usually eight to ten years after the disease began. Loss of ability to remember recent events is especially prominent. New material cannot be learned with the efficiency that previously was present, and eventually it cannot be learned at all. Deficient concentration, judgment, and, often emotional control become more and more prominent as the disease progresses.

For victims and their loved ones alike, the dementias are devastating. That cannot be glossed over. However, from our experience we have learned that the more families understand about the illness facing them, the better they are able to safeguard themselves against its worst effects. Some families even thrive despite their adversity. This book is aimed at providing the factual basis for that understanding.

The problems of the affected persons and their families are enormous. How should family members deal with an affected person? What medical treatments are available? What is wrong, anyhow? Is it only stubbornness? He, or she, seems perfectly able to remember some things "when it suits." What about driving? managing money? being left alone? drinking? danger because of carelessness with fire? assaultiveness? And most important, what can be expected as the disease progresses? Some families know that more than one member has been affected; therefore they suspect a genetic component, which adds greatly to the anxiety.

Answers to these and many other questions are not easily found. Usually it takes several weeks of visits to doctors plus a hospitalization or two before a diagnosis will even tentatively be suggested. Until quite recently, medical authorities ascribed mental decline to *hardening of the arteries* or arteriosclerosis of the vessels supplying blood to the brain. Now we know that they were wrong, but then it seemed to matter little because there was no effective treatment whether the assigned cause was correct or not. What was worse, no one could give an authoritative prediction—a prognosis—about what was likely to happen so that families could make realistic plans.

Planning was hard enough anyhow. Social service agencies could give limited material help and little useful information. The increasing numbers of the aged overwhelmed the services available and despite efforts, at times heroic efforts, planning often was not efficient. Moreover, dementing clients tended to be troublesome. They became confused and were often wanderers, straying from nursing homes and thereby creating a difficult problem which few homes were able to manage.

The picture has been changing. The brain sciences have been making extremely rapid progress and much more attention is being given to the illnesses of later life and their consequences. Exact medical diagnosis has become critically important because treatable diseases have been found hidden within the mass of dementias. Increasingly, there is reason for optimism about the future prospects for specific treatments of the remaining illnesses causing dementia. Much has been learned about the provision of medical and nursing care to dementing persons which is available today and is routinely applied in many centers. While the outlook is far from a happy one, it is brighter than it was a few years ago and it is steadily getting brighter.

For several years our medical research program in the genetics of dementing illness has brought us into close contact with persons with dementia and their families. Also, we have been seeing patients with dementing illnesses for diagnostic work-ups and treatment in clinics and in hospitals. One of our clinics at the University of Minnesota Hospital is devoted to providing information to families about the role of genetic factors in mental illnesses including the dementias. We have become well acquainted with dementia and its personal, financial and societal consequences.

Through our experiences, we have gained a store of practical information that we believe will be valuable to those who must deal with the dementias. We have aimed our book at the lay reader who will, we think, find the material understandable with little effort. That effort should be rewarded by acquisition of a good working grasp of the essential features of dementing illness. With that knowledge, the reader will have the facts needed to rationally plan and ease the burdens of those suffering from dementing illness and of those who love them.

Leonard L. Heston
June A. White

# CHAPTER 1
# DEMENTIA: THE SIGNS AND SYMPTOMS

The natural history of a disease is the story of its typical course over a period of time. It is as important as anything else we can learn about the disease. Nothing sets the natural history in mind so firmly as a description of a typical case. The description following is based on a composite picture of three persons suffering with dementing illnesses, whom we knew very well.

## A CASE OF DEMENTING ILLNESS

Harry D. seemed in perfect health at age fifty-eight, except that for a couple of days he had had a touch of flu. He worked in the municipal water treatment plant of a small city, and there, while responding to a minor emergency, Harry seemed to become confused about the order in which the levers controlling the flow of fluids were to be pulled. Several thousand gallons of raw sewage was discharged into a river. Harry had been an efficient and diligent worker and after puzzled questioning, his error was overlooked. Then, several weeks later, he came home with a baking dish that his wife had asked him to pick up; he had forgotten that he had brought the identical dish home two nights before. Later that month, on two successive nights, he went to pick up his daughter at her job in a restaurant, apparently forgetting that she had changed shifts and was working days. A week later he quite uncharacteristically became argumentative with a clerk at the phone company; he was trying to pay a bill that he had already paid three days before.

By this time his wife had become alarmed about the changes in Harry. When she discovered that he had been writing little notes to himself on odd scraps of paper, to serve as reminders, and that these included detailed instructions about how to operate machinery at work if various problems arose, she insisted that he see a doctor. Harry himself realized that his memory had been failing for perhaps as long as a year and he reluctantly agreed with his wife. The doctor did a physical examination and ordered several laboratory examinations, plus an electroencephalogram (a brain wave test). The examination results were normal and the doctor thought that the problem might be depression. He prescribed an antidepressant drug but, if anything, it seemed to make Harry's memory worse. It certainly did not make him feel better. Then the doctor thought that Harry had hardening of the arteries of the brain.

Months passed and Harry's wife was beside herself. Now fully aware of the problem, she could see that it was worsening. Not only had she been unable to get effective help, but Harry himself was becoming resentful and even suspicious of her attempts. He now insisted there was nothing at all wrong with him and she would catch him watching her every movement. From time to time he accused her of having the police watch him. He would draw all of the blinds in the house and once he ripped the telephone out of the wall; it was "spying." These episodes were tolerable because they were short lived; besides, there didn't seem to be dangerous intensity to any of Harry's ideas. His wife, who had the summer off from her position as a fourth grade teacher, began checking on him at his job at least once a day. Soon she was actually doing most of his work; his supervisor, an old friend of the family, looked the other way. Harry seemed to be very grateful that his wife was there.

Approximately eighteen months had passed since Harry had first allowed the sewage to escape and he was clearly a changed man. Most of the time he seemed preoccupied; he had a vacant smile on his face and what little he said seemed empty of meaning.

He had entirely given up his main interests, golf and woodworking. Sometimes he became angry—sudden storms of anger without apparent cause. This was quite unlike him. He would shout angrily at his wife and occasionally would throw or kick things, although his actions never seemed directed at anyone. He became careless about his person, and more and more he slept in his clothes. Gradually his wife took over—getting him up, toileted and dressed each morning.

Harry himself still insisted that nothing at all was wrong, but by now no one tried to explain things to him. He had long since stopped reading; he would sit vacantly in front of the television. He was no longer suspicious of television, but neither could he describe any program that he had watched. One day the county supervisor stopped by to tell Harry's wife that Harry just could not work any longer. He would be sixty-two in a few months and was eligible for early retirement. Of course he hadn't really worked for a long while anyhow, and he had become so inattentive that he was a hazard around the machinery.

Slowly Harry's condition worsened. He stayed alone at home through the day since his wife's school was in session. Sometimes he would wander out. He would greet everyone he met, old friends and strangers alike, with "Hi, it's so nice." That was the extent of his conversation, although he might repeat "nice, nice, nice . . ." over and over again. He had promised not to drive, but one day he did take the family automobile out and, fortunately, promptly got lost. The police brought him home; his wife took the keys to the automobile and kept them. When he left a coffee pot on a unit of the electric stove until it melted, his wife, who by this time was desperate for any help, took him to see another doctor. Again, Harry was found to be in good health. This time, however, the doctor ordered a "CAT" scan (computed axial tomography). This is a very sophisticated X ray examination which we will describe in Chapter 5. Using it, the doctor could visualize Harry's brain. The X ray showed that Harry's brain had actually shrunk in size; its diameter was a good two and one-half centimeters (about an inch) less than normal. The doctor said that Harry had "Pick's–Alzheimer Disease" and that there was no known cure or treatment.

Harry could no longer be left at home alone, so his daughter began working nights and caring for him during the day until his wife came home after school. He would sit all day, but sometimes he would wander aimlessly. He seemed to have no memory at all for events of the day and very little recollection of occasions from the distant past, which a year or so before he had enjoyed describing. His speech consisted of repetitions of the same word or phrase over and over, for example, "Hooky then, hooky then, hooky then." His wife tried and tried to find help. She was told the state mental hospitals did not "have a program that would meet his needs"; therefore, they "encouraged community facilities to care for chronic cases" such as Harry's.

Because Harry was a veteran, she took him to the nearest Veteran's Administration Hospital, which was 150 miles away. After a stay of nine weeks during which the CAT scan and all of the other tests were repeated with the same results, the doctors said that Harry had a chronic brain syndrome. They advised long-term hospitalization in a regional veterans hospital about 400 miles away from Harry's home. Meanwhile, his wife, who wanted Harry closer to home, had found that local nursing homes would charge almost 50 percent more than her monthly salary to care for Harry. Medicare would not pay for nursing home care. Social security and veteran's pension which Harry was now somehow eligible for (she was not sure why), would cover about one-third of the cost of a nursing home. But a visit to the home convinced her that the care provided was terribly inadequate. She could not manage Harry and apparently no one else would. Desperate, five years after the accident at work, she accepted with gratitude hospitalization at the veterans hospital which was so far away.

The nursing staff at the hospital sat Harry up in a chair each day and, aided by volunteers, made sure that he ate enough. Still he lost weight and became weaker. When his wife came to see him he would weep, but he did not talk and he gave no other sign that he recognized her. After a year he stopped weeping. His wife could no longer bear to visit. He lived on until just after his sixty-fifth birthday when he choked on some food, developed pneumonia, and died.

## SIGNS AND SYMPTOMS

Medical students are warned by their mentors, with a certain grim jocularity, to beware of *medical student's disease.* As students first learn the signs and symptoms of diseases, they are prone to discover those signs and symptoms in themselves, their friends and their relatives. The lesson seems simple: "Do not let subjective factors, especially emotions, influence your assessment of signs and symptoms." But in practice, maintaining objectivity can be extremely difficult.

Because dementia begins with forgetfulness, something we all experience too often, it is especially likely to lead any of us to err. When evaluating an instance of forgetfulness, we may, on the one hand, exaggerate its importance and experience a flash of unwarranted worry about ourselves or others, or, on the other, minimize it and fail to recognize developing illness. After all, Harry's accident at the water treatment plant and his early lapses of memory are not utterly alien to experiences any of us might have had in life. Such occasional lapses of memory are well within the limits of normality. It is the continual, marked and irreversible loss of memory that spells illness. It can be very hard to recognize the difference between normal lapses and disease, especially when the disease is just beginning.

For persons emotionally attached to victims of a dementing process, the early stages of the illness may place them in an extremely upsetting whipsaw. Because the early signs can sometimes be seen in normals, and become signs of illness only when seen too often or too intensely, we may too readily explain signs of illness in others, especially loved ones. Depending on our mood or general outlook, we may exaggerate the importance of signs such as failure to remember in ourselves—"am I getting senile?" or discount it in others—"he can remember the things he wants to remember." We may also use opposing fallacies and come to opposite conclusions. Thus we may find ourselves pulled back and forth, sometimes minimizing objectively alarming signs of illness and sometimes overvaluing the importance of normal everyday lapses. This whipsawing is typical, normal, but terribly painful for families facing dementing illness. Even doctors, who are rigorously trained to counteract such subjective, emotionally laden reasoning are sometimes victims of it. For the lay person trying to understand a loved one, perfect objectivity is impossible. But we must try.

Memory loss such as Harry experienced is so central to dementia, and objective understanding is so important, that we will discuss it several times as we proceed. It therefore will be helpful to understand some general features of memory formation. Although quite a lot is known about some conditions affecting memory, the exact mechanism of memory formation is also one of the major unsolved problems of neuroscience and biology generally. One critical distinction important in dementia is that between *short-term* or *immediate* memory, and *long-term* or *distant* memory.

We retain enough information about our immediate environment and its very recent history to allow us to monitor it continuously and adjust our responses accordingly. However, most of this material is not stored in long-term memory. Rather, it is quickly forgotten as it obviously must be; otherwise, our storage capacity would soon be overwhelmed. For example, we can usually, though with effort, recall what we had for breakfast today, but we probably will be unable to remember what we had yesterday. Why should we? This information would be most unlikely to be of value to us. Long-term memory apparently is first established as short-term memory but then other brain mechanisms must become involved. Although the mechanism of this process is unknown, some conditions which govern its regulation, and which promote or retard the formation of long-term memory, are known. Both voluntary and involuntary processes are apparently involved.

We remember that which seems to be important or that which is associated with some important emotion or event. If we should become ill after breakfast, or if while eating we should learn from the morning paper that we had won the Irish Sweepstakes, we would be more likely to remember what we had eaten. We can also establish long-term memory by making special effort. For example, we can memorize nonsense symbols and retain them in memory indefinitely if we make unnatural efforts. We remember important facts for long periods and our memory is helped if the facts are occasionally recalled and used. The vocabulary of a foreign language provides a good example of this process. Emotionally important or stressful events may be retained in long-term memory, whether we want them there or not. Likewise, several factors interfere with the establishment of long-term memory. Emotional arousal appears to inhibit the formation of memories which are not directly related to the cause of the arousal. (Lovers may be oblivious to everything around them, yet have very intense memories.) Alcohol interferes with memory and so do many other commonly used drugs. We will later discuss these and other such impediments more extensively.

The first sign of dementing illness is loss of recent memory, with the relative preservation of long-term memory. A wedding or highschool football game may be correctly recalled in great detail by a person who cannot retain enough immediate memory to allow him to count change after a purchase. The same person may remember an emotionally charged event that occurred a week before, but be unable to converse about the news of the day.

Harry's history illustrates the importance of the distinction between immediate and long-term memory. He could manage routine operations on his job, but when he had to deal with a minor emergency that no doubt required that he retain enough recent memory to be able to perform effectively while deviating from routine, his disability became evident. Likewise, he managed to pick up his daughter as long as doing so was a nightly routine. When the routine changed, Harry failed to adapt.

Harry's failures in these respects introduce an important concept, the *threshold.* It is not unusual for a major illness to appear to begin with a flu, as in Harry's case, or with some other illness or accident. The brain and other organs have reserve capacities beyond that which is needed to cope with ordinary demands. If that reserve capacity is gradually lost to disease, the loss may go unnoticed until a stress such as the flu makes added demands, even minor ones, which cannot be met. Then a marginal adaptation may abruptly be lost.

An example might be helpful. In normal healthy life, about 40–45 percent of the volume of blood is taken up by red blood cells, which carry oxygen. Given ordinary levels of physical activity, a gradual loss of cells until they comprise a much smaller proportion of the total volume, say 20–25 percent, may go unnoticed; but then strenuous activity or an illness, both of which increase the body's requirement for oxygen, or even moving to a higher altitude where less oxygen is available, may precipitate major signs of illness such as heart failure. The threshold was crossed. Such challenges to our capacities are a part of normal life. We cannot avoid acknowledging disease by pretending that the challenge caused the problem.

These relationships can be quite confusing for families who naturally try to attach a *cause* to illness. More importantly, we have seen guilt for causing illness wrongly assumed or assigned: "If only I hadn't made him go out in the rain" or "Our son was such a worry to him." We seek understandable explanations and too easily accept the one that seems most likely. When searching to explain illness, we are most often wrong.

Only slightly less noticeable than loss of recent memory, as the disease progresses, is the diminution in the logical and social capacities which we group together and describe as *judgment.* We continuously respond to challenges from our environment. As we have seen, doing this requires that we obtain information about our environment, integrate it into our consciousness, and make responses or choose not to respond. We thus exercise judgment.

Dementing persons are not able to assimilate information with the efficiency they exhibited before becoming ill, and therefore, their responses are less adept. At first, the deficits may be noticeable only in the nuances of social deportment; for example, the dementing person may be uncharacteristically inattentive to the conversation. The whole context of social situations is not grasped with the facility previously exhibited, and hence the quality of the reactions is worse than before. Here too, long-established patterns of behavior which have become effectively automatic tend to be preserved. It is the new situation involving new people, new facts, a new environment which makes the developing disability evident.

The relative preservation of old skills can be deceptive. For example, communication skills tend to be preserved. A verbally fluent person can continue to produce grammatically correct sentences using a large vocabulary despite a moderately advanced dementia. It is only when one looks for the meaning in the communication, and compares it with the quality the affected person was previously capable of achieving, that the disability becomes evident.

Closely related to judgment is ability to abstract, and this capacity too declines precipitously. Finding common themes, sorting important from unimportant details—these are examples of abstracting abilities that rapidly become impaired. Again, the loss can be difficult to detect in one who has spent a lifetime dealing with abstract ideas. The same words and phrases that served well before illness developed may be repeated and may sound superficially convincing. Only close examination may reveal the underlying vagueness and poverty of thought.

Emotionality is yet another major capacity showing progressive impairment, though usually after the loss of memory has become evident. Early in the course, two conflicting tendencies may be observed, often in the same person. We may observe a decrease in emotional responsiveness leading to an apparently apathetic uninvolvement with events—a flatness of gesture, tone of voice, and facial expression. However, these changes often exist simultaneously with a heightened responsiveness that may be quite alien to the previous personality. Hypersexuality, coarsening of humor, irritability, and sometimes physical striking out may appear. As the disease progresses, the apathy and uninvolvement comes to dominate.

Harry exhibited such behaviors. Early in his course he exhibited some emotional lability, especially temper outbursts. He was typically ineffective. He didn't hurt anyone because his outbursts were short lived and not really targeted. Underlying these changes in behavior, Harry became more suspicious, generally *paranoid* in his outlook. This, too, is a fairly common development in dementia. While it can be quite troublesome, in most cases the erroneous ideas and unfounded suspicions are held only briefly, and do not seem to generate much emotional fervor behind actions based on them. This was true of Harry. Later, he became totally unresponsive. Looked at in perspective over the course of his illness, the changes in his behavior marked unmistakable and irreversible stages in the destruction of his personality.

As Harry's history illustrates, the diseases causing dementia progress at a fairly steady rate with no periods of improvement. Memory decline remains the salient sign of progressive illness. While immediate memory remains relatively more severely impaired, long-term memory also eventually becomes affected. In response to questions, a past event may be recalled, but the description becomes poorer in details and finally, only unintelligible nonsense phrases are produced. Later, as in Harry's case, members of the immediate family are not recognized. Communication of any kind becomes rarer and, toward the end, it effectively ceases. The occasional bursts of emotion have given way to a pervasive apathy and finally no response of any degree can be observed. The affected person becomes physically less active. More time is spent staring off into vacant space.

Late in the course, there may be changes in the nervous control of muscles. These changes most often produce rigidity due to increased muscle tone (hypertonicity). Because of the rigidity, it may become difficult to bring food to the mouth and the patient may need to be fed. Rigidity may also produce painful cramping which is often especially troublesome at night. Eventually, the illness will advance until the affected person is bedfast.

Also late in the course, seizures (epileptic fits) may develop. These usually take the form of rapid alternating movements of arms or legs or both. Urine or feces may be involuntarily lost and generally a brief period of unconsciousness follows. Seizures are alarming to those unused to seeing them. However, they are usually quite harmless when they appear as a feature of dementing illness and much less distressing than cramps to the ill person. Later, in Chapter 6, we will discuss treatments of these effects of the illness.

Just before the last stages are reached, there is often a substantial loss of weight. Most victims will have to be fed. If loss of control of bladder and bowel has not occurred during the previous months, it certainly will at this time. Skilled nursing care will generally be required to prevent bed sores from becoming a major problem. Death, six to eight years after onset, on the average, is not directly due to dementing illness. Pneumonia, kidney infection, or choking on food are the direct causes. The real cause is one of the cruelest diseases to assail the human spirit.

# CHAPTER 2

# DISEASES PRODUCING PRIMARY DEMENTIA

Several distinct diseases which can produce a course and outcome like Harry's will be the subject of this chapter. Distinguishing these diseases one from the other is most important to patients, their families, and their doctors. Some of them can be treated or even cured; obviously, these must be recognized without delay. The different diseases have different natural histories. They may differ in average age at onset, average length of illness, or other features such as muscular control. Some dementing illnesses carry genetic risks which family members will want to know about. Knowing which disease is present allows families to plan accordingly.

Genetic risks have a special and paradoxically hopeful aspect. As we shall see, there are excellent reasons to believe that successful treatments for some of the dementing illnesses will be developed over the next decades. Then rapid diagnosis, which is often most difficult to accomplish, will become extremely important. Accurate diagnosis must precede treatment because the different diseases will surely respond to different treatments. A correct diagnosis for at least one member of the family will help any other family member showing signs of illness. The laws of probability and genetics make it extremely likely that all affected members of one family will have the same illness. In cases where the illness is dementia, we have never observed an exception. Whenever two cases were observed in one family, the final diagnosis was the same for both. Therefore, a working diagnosis could be made in light of family history, and specific treatment begun immediately.

Understanding the dementing illnesses will be made much easier if we first separate them along natural dividing lines into three groups: primary undifferentiated dementia, primary differentiated dementia, and secondary dementia. In the following sections, we will discuss the first two groups, which are known as *progressive dementias,* in detail. The secondary dementias are described in Chapter 3 along with other diseases and conditions which may look like progressive dementia, but which may often be successfully treated and are most important for that reason.

## PRIMARY UNDIFFERENTIATED DEMENTIAS

This group includes diseases which primarily affect the brain and produce dementia through direct effects on brain tissue. The diseases in this group resemble one another quite closely and generally cannot be distinguished by ordinary diagnostic procedures. A direct examination of brain tissue, usually obtained by an autopsy, is required. Alzheimer's dementia, Pick's disease and other extremely rare or so far unclassified diseases belong in this group. Harry had one of them. These are the diseases which are the major concern of this book.

### DEMENTIA OF THE ALZHEIMER TYPE

Alzheimer's disease, or dementia of the Alzheimer type, is the most common dementing illness. It affects 20–30 percent of the population who reach their mid-eighties, and it accounts for about half of the cases of dementia at any age. It was named after a German physician, Alios Alzheimer, who identified and described it in 1907. Dr. Alzheimer described changes which he saw in his microscope in brain tissue from a person who had an illness similar to Harry's. Those changes were not present in brain tissues from normal persons. Because of their appearance under the microscope, the changes were named *neurofibrillary tangles* and *senile plaques.* These were seen to occur associated with neurons, or nerve cells.

The changes described by Alzheimer may occur in most parts of the brain, but they tend to occur in greatest numbers in the part of the brain which is involved with memory, the hippocampus. A valid diagnosis of an Alzheimer dementia requires the visualization under the microscope of the same changes in brain tissue originally described by Dr. Alzheimer. Since we obviously cannot, except in exceptional circumstances, remove a portion of the brain for such examination from a living person, we cannot be certain of the diagnosis unless we perform this examination in autopsy.

The nerve cells or neurons which are being destroyed in Alzheimer's dementia are the working components of the brain. From them comes the commands which set our muscles into motion. They contain our memories, receive the sights and sounds of our surroundings, cause our hormones to be secreted and produce our emotions. Nerve tissue affected by tangles or plaques looks dead. Obviously a brain containing many of them is not functioning well enough to interpret life in all of its richness or to mount a human response to it.

Figure 2.1 shows what brain tissue looks like under the microscope. The brain above contains the plaques and tangles characteristic of Alzheimer's dementia. A normal brain is below. The legend to the figure explains the important differences.

Although aged primates may develop a few plaques, the combination of plaques and tangles, as in Figure 2.1 above, is seen only in humans. This particular disease-caused change in tissue, unlike nearly any other, seems to be unique to our species. However, we do find plaques and tangles in other human conditions: mainly, normal aging and Down's syndrome. A few brain cells in most of us will develop such changes provided we live to fairly advanced ages—into our mid-seventies. Plaques and tangles are widely scattered in ordinary aging, quite unlike the myriads of affected cells seen in Alzheimer's disease. A few such scattered cells do not significantly impair memory or thinking. Nevertheless, this possible link with normal aging is regarded as an important clue to both Alzheimer's dementia and aging.

Down's syndrome or mongolism is another condition in which plaques and tangles appear in large numbers, indistinguishable from Alzheimer's dementia itself, but the age at onset is much younger, nearly always before age forty. Apparently a very large proportion of Down's cases, perhaps approaching 100 percent, who live to that age, develop Alzheimer's dementia. Their skills

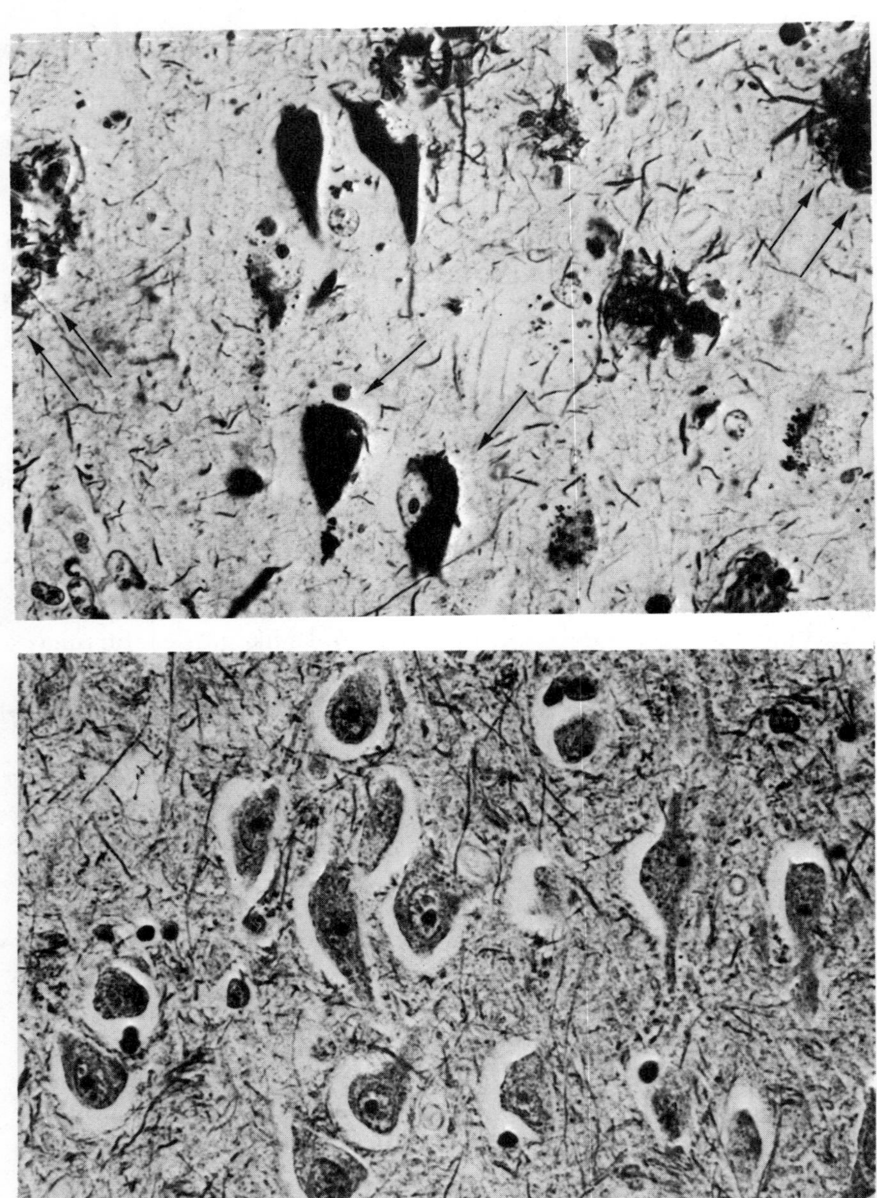

*Figure 2.1* **Alzheimer's Disease: Microscopic Changes in Brain Tissue**
The brain tissue shown above is from a patient with Alzheimer's disease. The single arrows point to *tangles* and double arrows to typical examples of *senile plaque*. The normal brain tissue shown below contains no such structures. Magnification 550×. Courtesy of Dr. Angeline R. Mastri.

are severely limited by mental retardation throughout life, but they lose even those, and plaques and tangles are found in their brains after death. Down's syndrome, which is associated with mental retardation present from birth, may seem oddly out of place when the subject is dementia in otherwise normal adults, but there are curious links between the two conditions which may provide other valuable clues to researchers.

An unfortunate confusion in terminology which became established in the years after Alzheimer wrote must be cleared before continuing. Today one cannot read far into the literature of the subject before encountering it. The illness Alzheimer described became divided into two diagnoses: Alzheimer's disease and senile dementia. The course of both was similar and the changes in brain were indistinguishable. Nevertheless, two terms were used: Alzheimer's disease, if the onset of illness was at or before age sixty-five; senile dementia, if the onset was after age sixty-five.

There is an understandable historical basis for this division of one thing into two without sufficient evidence, but there is no logical reason for continuing to do so. Today, Alzheimer's disease and senile dementia are regarded as one disease. Over the last few years, both terms have been discarded in formal communication in favor of *Dementia of the Alzheimer Type,* abbreviated DAT or, alternatively, *Senile Dementia of the Alzheimer Type,* abbreviated SDAT. We will use DAT in this book. Pending discovery of further evidence, we assume the basic disease process is the same, regardless of age at onset.

The age at which DAT begins is, however, a clue to the degree of severity of the illness, not only in persons affected, but also in their families as a whole. It is, of course, very difficult to estimate precisely the age at which a dementing illness begins. The onset is extremely insidious. Therefore, by convention, age of onset is operationally defined as the age at which deficits in recent memory first become irreversibly established. In Harry's case, this would be when he brought home the baking dish for the second time, closely followed by his failure to remember his daughter's change of schedule. Such definitions are crude but they are the best available.

In Table 2.1, the ages at onset of a series of DAT cases can be seen.

Note that early onset tends to be associated with a shorter duration of illness. This is consistent with medicine's general experi-

*TABLE 2.1 Age at Onset Related to Survival in DAT*

| AGE AT ONSET (YRS.) | PERCENT WITH ONSET | CUMULATIVE PERCENT | AVERAGE SURVIVAL (YRS.) | LONGEST SURVIVAL (YRS.) |
|---|---|---|---|---|
| –44 | 3 | 3 | 4.5 | 6 |
| 45–49 | 2 | 5 | 6.1 | 9.9 |
| 50–54 | 5 | 10 | 7.2 | 12.2 |
| 55–59 | 7 | 17 | 8.5 | 16.1 |
| 60–64 | 14 | 31 | 8.4 | 25.2 |
| 65–69 | 19 | 50 | 8.5 | 18.1 |
| 70–74 | 17 | 67 | 8.4 | 21.3 |
| 75–79 | 18 | 85 | 6.1 | 11.9 |
| 80–84 | 10 | 95 | 5.0 | 13.4 |
| 85– | 5 | 100 | 4.1 | 8.3 |

ence with chronic diseases. The earlier the onset, the more severe the illness and therefore, the shorter its course. Through the middle range of onset ages, from fifty-five to seventy, the average remaining period of life is quite consistent, around 8.5 years. This information is useful in planning, but note also the last column, *longest survival.* Though such cases are rare, we have reasonably well-documented periods of survival which are quite prolonged. Onset at more advanced ages is again associated with shorter periods of survival on the average. As age advances, of course, other diseases which cause death, such as cancer or heart disease, become more likely. That effect is sufficient to account for the observed shorter survival.

As an example of the use of Table 2.1, suppose that onset was at age fifty-seven years and six months. Then we can see that 7 percent of all DAT cases begin between ages fifty-five–fifty-nine and that our case is among the 17 percent which begin before the sixtieth birthday is reached. We can anticipate an average survival of 8.5 years after onset or to age sixty-six in this case (57.5 + 8.5). However, survival might be nearly twice that long or shorter.

## PICK'S DISEASE

In life, Pick's disease appears much like DAT. Attempts to distinguish it from DAT in living patients, without direct examination of brain tissue, have not been successful. Based on the evidence presented, Harry could have had Pick's disease or DAT or others among the illnesses we shall subsequently discuss. An exact diagnosis is possible only by examination of brain tissue. Under the microscope, those differences are profound. Figure 2.2 shows a microscopic slice of brain tissue from a case of Pick's disease.

The affected cells have *Pick's bodies,* which apparently consist of a miscellaneous collection of parts of the normal cell in disarray. The parts are recognizable, but normal relationships among them have been lost. The appearance is utterly different from what we saw in the brain in Figure 2.1 from a case of DAT. Therefore, we

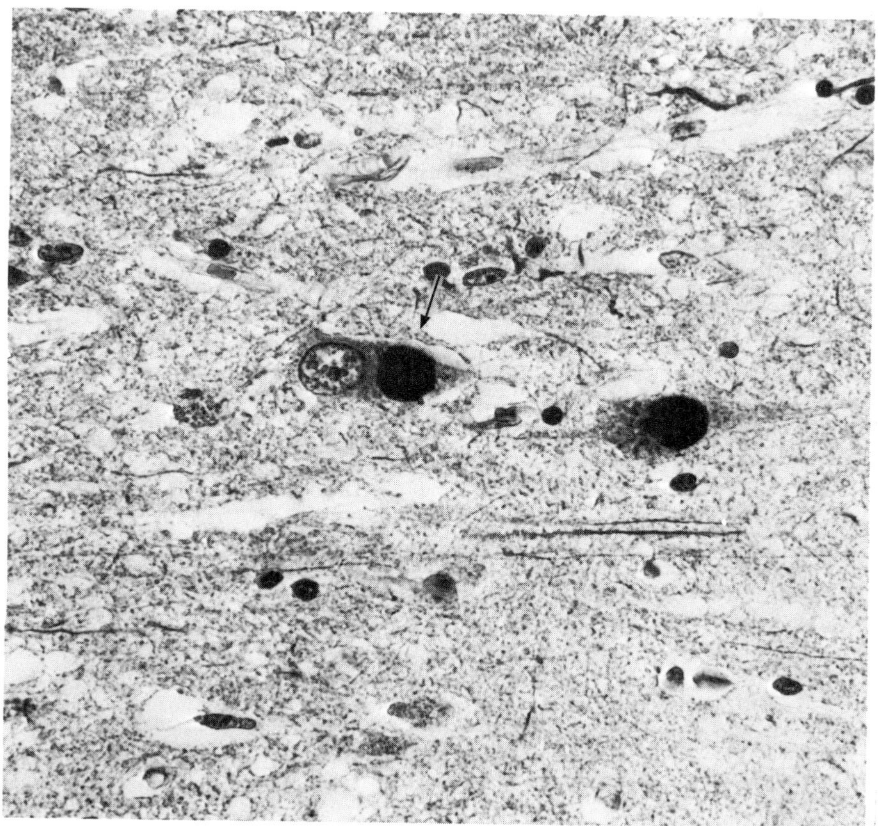

*Figure 2.2* **Pick's Disease: Microscopic Changes in Brain Tissue**
A brain section from a case of Pick's disease. The arrow indicates a typical Pick inclusion in a nerve cell. Note how this brain differs from DAT. (Figure 2.1). Magnification 550×. Courtesy of Dr. Angeline R. Mastri.

presume that the disease that produced the pathology must also be different, and effective treatments, when they appear, surely will be different.

The natural history and course of Pick's disease is not as well known as that of DAT. On the average, the onset can be reasonably estimated as 55.4 years with death following 7 years later. Table 2.2 shows how age at onset and severity of illness are related. Table 2.2 is based on only 39 cases; therefore, the relationships depicted are not nearly as strong as seen in Table 2.1, which was based on 200 DAT cases.

There is another important clue in Table 2.2. After ages in the mid-fifties, new cases of Pick's become infrequent, and only three cases of Pick's with onset over age seventy have been reported. Pick's disease and DAT have been reported as beginning at ages in the early twenties, but that is extremely rare.

Pick's is much less frequent than DAT at any age, but its importance to diagnostic assessment must not be underestimated. Pick's cases are concentrated in age ranges where they are likely to be confused with the small proportion of DAT cases which begin at relatively youthful ages. This is important because youthful onset is associated with relatively more severe diseases. Greater severity implies greater risk to relatives and suggests more flagrant biochemical or physiological faults. It is precisely these early-onset cases that are most important to families and medical scientists alike. Unclassified dementias also complicate diagnosis in early-onset cases.

## UNCLASSIFIED DEMENTIAS

DAT and Pick's are markedly different when we look at brain tissue. However, there are other diseases and processes, no one can

***TABLE 2.2 Age at Onset Related to Survival in Pick's Disease***

| AGE AT ONSET (YRS.) | PERCENT | CUMULATIVE PERCENT | AVERAGE SURVIVAL (YRS.) | LONGEST SURVIVAL (YRS.) |
|---|---|---|---|---|
| –39 | 7 | 7 | 4.5 | 4.5 |
| 40–49 | 13 | 20 | 6.9 | 8.1 |
| 50–59 | 38 | 58 | 7.4 | 8.0 |
| 60–69 | 28 | 86 | 7.6 | 8.8 |
| 70– | 14 | 100 | 7.2 | 7.4 |

say how many, which produce dementia indistinguishable in life from that produced by DAT or Pick's. That is, in any moderately large number of cases which in life will meet all of the criteria of a primary dementia, complete brain tissue examination will prove them to be neither DAT, Pick's, nor any other specific disease or process. Such cases, which we will call *unclassified dementias,* are a measure of our ignorance. Some such cases are probably depressions; others are probably extremely rare diseases or unusual variants of more common diseases. Separation of diseases by explicit criteria is a fundamental task of medical research. It is far from adequate in the dementias.

The unclassified dementias are of particular importance because, in our experience, most of them begin in the middle decades of life and hence are easily confused with Pick's and those cases of DAT which begin relatively early. Table 2.3 presents the relative frequency of DAT, Pick's and the unclassified dementias according to age at onset.

Given a case of primary dementia, with age at onset estimated with reasonable accuracy, one can obtain from Table 2.3 an estimate of the probability of the three listed causes. For example, a case with onset at age fifty-nine or before has a probability of 0.59 of being DAT, 0.20 of Pick's and 0.20 of unclassified dementia.

These proportions are important. Because diagnosis based on direct examination of brain is so difficult to obtain, much of the research in the dementias has been based on the assumption that DAT constitutes such a preponderance of all dementias that other causes can safely be neglected. Obviously from Table 2.3, this is just not so. Moreover, the stakes are quite high. All medical experience says that when tissue changes are as distinctive as illustrated in Figures 2.1 and 2.2 for DAT and Pick's, different causes will be at work and different effective treatments eventually will be found.

***Table 2.3*** ***Proportions of Primary Dementias with Onset in Indicated Age Intervals***

| AGE INTERVAL | PROBABILITY OF DAT (%) | PROBABILITY OF PICK'S (%) | PROBABILITY OF UNCLASSIFIED (%) |
|---|---|---|---|
| –59 | 59 | 20 | 20 |
| 60–69 | 79 | 10 | 10 |
| 70–79 | 93 | 3 | 3 |
| 80– | 100 | – | – |

Lumping all dementias together is doomed to lead to false conclusions. When evaluating research results, the reader must always ask: "How was the diagnosis established?"

## NORMAL PRESSURE HYDROCEPHALUS (NPH)

This most important disorder, which is also known as *low pressure hydrocephalus* (LPH), or *water on the brain,* may account for as many as 5 percent of mid-life dementias. It occupies an uncertain position with respect to the diseases we have so far considered. However, we believe it is more closely related to the primary undifferentiated dementias than to any other diagnostic group.

In 1968, psychiatrists and neurologists were cheered by news that a cause of a form of dementia had been discovered which, best of all, was treatable by a surgical operation. Doctors eagerly searched for patients who matched the published descriptions. Some were found and operated upon with great benefit. It is still clear that this disease does cause some dementias, and that in these cases, the surgical treatment is indeed effective. The early optimism, however, has been greatly tempered by unhappy results in a significant proportion of cases.

Normal pressure hydrocephalus (NPH) involves impaired circulation of spinal fluid. Spinal fluid (often abbreviated CSF) is a clear colorless fluid related to lymph. It is secreted into compartments within the brain called ventricles; these are filled with CSF. There are four ventricles, two small and midline in the brain, and two large on either side of the midline. The latter two are called *lateral ventricles.* CSF is secreted within the lateral ventricles, moves rearward through the midline ventricles, and then goes through three small apertures to the outer surface of the brain. It bathes the surface of the brain and the spinal cord and is finally reabsorbed by special structures on the surface of the brain, which return it to the circulating blood, through veins which drain into the jugular vein.

Several diseases are produced by disturbance of the production, circulation or resorption of CSF. Hydrocephalus can be produced by obstruction of flow between the place where CSF is produced in the lateral ventricles and where it is absorbed on the surface of the brain. Between the lateral ventricles and the obstruction, pressure will be increased, at least initially. The pressure destroys brain tissue and, in infants, may even deform the skull. In NPH there is no mechanical obstruction to the flow of CSF, and hence no increase in fluid pressure. The pressure is normal or, in comparison to the pressures present in obstruction, even low—hence the names given the condition.

There are at least two types of NPH. One type occurs following injury or infection, sometimes years later. In such cases, the hydrocephalus may partly be due to impaired absorption of CSF due to tissue destroyed by the original injury. This occurs often after a hemorrhage of blood into the CSF, but the mechanism is by no means completely understood. At any rate, the onset of dementia is not unlike Harry's, but the progression usually is more rapid, and there is a history of previous injury to the brain. In addition, and most important, NPH tends strongly to produce disturbance in standing and walking (station and gait to the neurologist), or urinary incontinence, or both. These problems come early in the course of the illness. In DAT, Pick's, and the other primary dementias, gait disturbance and incontinence may appear, but generally quite late in the course of those illnesses.

Dementia, gait disturbance and incontinence also mark a second type of NPH, one which produces much the same effects but without a preceding injury to the brain. There is a further important difference between the two types of NPH. The type which follows injury can be greatly benefited by surgery. A small plastic tube is inserted through which CSF can flow from the ventricles directly to the jugular vein, bypassing the structures which absorb CSF. NPH which develops in the absence of injury is not so often benefited by surgery, and, because the surgery itself is risky, the decision to operate should be carefully considered by the operating surgeons, together with patients and their relatives.

NPH can be diagnosed with satisfactorily high probability in life and, because it is one of the few treatable causes of dementia, doctors are very sensitive to the possibility that it is present. The odds therefore favor correct diagnosis and treatment. The history of injury and the appearance of a disturbance in gait early in the course of illness are two important keys to correct diagnosis.

## PRIMARY DIFFERENTIATED DEMENTIA

The diseases in this group also primarily affect brain tissue, but they have features observable in life which usually, though not always, distinguish them from the primary undifferentiated group. The features which allow separation are mainly abnormal movements. Huntington's disease is the major entity in this group. These diseases are important because they may sometimes be wrongly diagnosed as an undifferentiated dementia. This group of diseases also will later provide us useful examples of genetic principles and of brain function. Groups A and B together are often called *progressive dementias* because the course of the illness is smoothly progressive, without abrupt peaks or valleys of improvement or worsening.

1. Huntington's disease is nearly always distinguished from other dementias by peculiar involuntary writhing movements which any physician can recognize in their typical form. Except that the diagnosis is usually easily made, Huntington's disease has much in common with the undifferentiated dementias, and most of what we shall say about them is also applicable to Huntington's.
2. Creutzfeldt-Jakob disease is an infectious disease due to a virus. It can generally be distinguished from other dementias by its relatively rapid course—months rather than years from onset to death, but this is not always the case. Sometimes the course is prolonged, and some undifferentiated dementias progress rapidly. Again, diagnosis requires an autopsy.

   Some families have several cases of this illness, suggesting that genetic factors may play a part in its occurrence. This would not be unusual. A genetic predisposition to viral illness seems to be fairly common in medicine. We will later discuss the possible contribution of viruses to other dementias.
3. There remain a miscellaneous collection of diseases which are individually very rare. Some have been described in only one family. Conceivably one such, progressive supranuclear palsy, could be confused with an undifferentiated dementia. The illness, however, must be very rare—we have never seen a case—and from the descriptions of it, a paralysis of certain eye movements (upward gaze) is a constant feature that should distinguish it from any other dementia. Another possible candidate is Wilson's disease. Nearly all cases of this rare illness begin with signs of liver disease. If the brain is involved, impairments of movement are the usual first signs. If mental processes become involved early in the course, confusion with primary dementia

could occur. A reasonably competent medical examination should arrive at a correct diagnosis in even the most unusual case.

That completes the list of brain diseases associated with progressive dementia which might possibly be confused with a primary undifferentiated dementia such as DAT or Pick's disease. However, there are further considerations. In the next chapter we take up other diseases and conditions which may produce a dementia or apparent dementia secondary to impairment of an organ other than the brain. These other diseases and conditions must be considered as possible causes of signs of dementia, even though the brain is not the seat of disease. Equally important, they must be considered as possible additions to an impairment produced by a primary disease of the brain and this possibility will also be an important aspect of the next chapter.

# CHAPTER 3

# DISEASES AND CONDITIONS ASSOCIATED WITH SECONDARY DEMENTIA

Signs of dementia may be associated with diseases which do not usually attack the brain directly. Disease in most organs of the body can produce significant effects on brain function. Heart and lung diseases are especially important in this respect. Many drugs or toxic substances can also seriously interfere with brain function. These conditions are important because they can mimic many effects of the primary dementias. Symptoms of dementia could possibly be caused by drugs, toxins, or disease of organs other than the brain. Moreover, disease of other organs or the effects of drugs may add to the impairment produced by primary brain disease. Any such addition may turn a mild impairment into an incapacitating one. Remember how Harry's flu was associated with increased signs of brain disease. Doctors and concerned nonprofessionals alike will be better able to help patients with signs of dementia if they understand these possibilities. A common cause of secondary dementia is depression.

## DEPRESSION

Depression, a psychiatric disorder, is one of the most common major illnesses of adult life. It can mimic dementing illness so closely that distinguishing between the two disorders can be extremely difficult. In fact, some persons who are only depressed die in institutions or nursing homes after years of illness wrongly regarded as dementia. This is rare, but can happen. We found three cases of depression among 158 cases which had been screened in life to include only dementia.

Since depression is very common, those three cases represent a vanishingly small proportion of the total number of depressions in the population from which they came. They were not typical examples of depression. They were those left over after nearly all depression had been recognized by the treating physicians. Such unrecognized cases occur in large part because of sheer numbers at risk. Approximately 30 percent of the population over age sixty-five will experience a major depression sometime during the next three years. In such a large population, some cases will be atypical and some of those will resemble dementia very closely. Misdiagnosis of such a few cases of depression represents a very small percentage error. It is understandable, given human limitations. But there should be none at all, because today complete recovery from depression not only is possible but is the rule. Everyone concerned should be working toward reducing the number of misdiagnosed cases to zero.

Depression presents further complications. Dementing illness usually features a depression sometime during its course. This often appears in the early stages, and it can be quite severe. Furthermore, some of the drugs taken by depressed persons, both by prescription and by over-the-counter purchase, can cause impairments of intellectual functions which can easily be confused with dementia. The problems are extremely complicated and, in difficult cases, a specialized physician will be needed to work out the diagnosis. Sometimes even experts cannot arrive at a certain diagnosis. Then doctors may advise that treatment for depression be started in the hope that it might be beneficial. The decision is not a reckless one, but rather reasonable, because depression can be treated successfully while most dementias cannot. This is giving the benefit of diagnostic doubts to the treatable condition.

Depression not only is important to our consideration of dementia, but is also an illness where the participation of families is most important in both diagnosis and treatment. The more families know, the better they will be able to help the diagnostic process along and to gauge its effectiveness. Therefore, we will explain depression in sufficient depth.

Depression is a disorder of mood. By mood we mean the prevailing feeling tone over a lengthy period of time—days rather than hours. Climate provides an apt analogy. We may correctly describe a climate as rainy and yet not be surprised at occasional sunshine. Similarly, a depressed mood is perfectly congruent with flashes of normality or even happiness. What counts is the average over a longer range. Variation in mood is normal. If good fortune falls to us, our mood tends to be high, while ill luck is followed by an opposite tendency. If there is a lot of ill luck or if an extremely sad event occurs—the death of a loved one, for example—the low mood will likely be deeper and longer lasting.

These normal variations are part of our common experience and so are understandable. We can put ourselves in another's place: "If that event (or those events) had happened to me, I would be just as low." We generally are not aware of making such an explicit test, but that appears to be the process we follow in assessing feeling states in others. Depressions, the most serious depressions in particular, usually occur without any antecedent event. They are described as *endogenous,* meaning that they arose within the affected person in the absence of any apparent external cause.

When depression is used as a medical diagnosis, the mood change is greater than could reasonably be explained by an external event, or the mood change has lasted longer than usual after a serious event. For example, the death of a spouse commonly produces a deeply depressed mood and is certainly sufficient explanation for such change. However, the mood should start to lighten after a few weeks and although pangs of depression may come for years at decreasing frequency (though not decreasing intensity), the reaction to the death should be effectively ended after a few months. Depressive illness should be suspected to be replacing a normal reaction when these limits are exceeded.

Mood tends to color all of our perceptions. In depression, a tinge of blackness colors all of our judgments and values. Our past memories, our future expectations, our families, our associations, everything we are seems blackened to a degree which depends on the depth of the depression. Every fault, real or imagined, is exaggerated. Negativism, guilt, and remorse preoccupy thinking. A doctor, after recovering from a depression, told us that he could not imagine a more painful disease except perhaps rabies.

Mood is a subjective state. We can describe our own mood, though sometimes with difficulty, but we must be told what mood others are experiencing; being told is the only direct evidence available to us. However, we are helped by several indirect indicators of mood. The affected person will seem preoccupied with negative aspects of his life. The blackness described above will usually dominate conversation. The facial expression will be sad most of the time. Don't be deceived by a few smiles. We smile through tears almost as much as we smile for joy, because smiling is such a ubiquitous, nonspecific human response. Depressed people often do not have the appetite to eat enough, and weight loss can be quite substantial—10–20 percent of body weight over a few weeks would not be unusual. There is often difficulty sleeping, especially sleeping through the night. A depressed person may go to bed at ordinary times and may fall asleep without undue difficulty, but then awaken after an hour or two and be unable to go back to sleep. Those early morning hours are the worst. In general, depression is at its worst on first awakening and then gets better as the day wears on, until by early evening the mood may be approaching normal, even in severely ill persons.

From what has been presented so far, it should be clear that most depressions could be readily separated from dementia. The problem in diagnosis is mainly due to a small minority of depressions that feature severe *retardation.* Retarded depression is so named because responses such as movements, thinking, and speech are slowed, often dramatically so. Sometimes there is hardly any speech. Words are separated by such long pauses that the listener may lose any sense of continuity. This, coupled with a vacant unchanging facial expresion and a generalized poverty of responses, can look very much like dementia. Some depressions have another deceptive feature. There may be an actual intellectual deficit which affects memory, abstracting ability and judgment. Successful treatment will reverse these deficits, but without treatment, they may look like early dementia.

Because depression is such a dramatic possibility when dementia is suspected, it is hard to avoid overvaluing signs, finding evidence of depression in every frown. It is true that many depressions will slip by a cursory medical examination, but not a competent one. Even if a depression goes unrecognized, the passage of time will usually bring enough improvement to eliminate dementia from consideration. Over a couple of months, nearly all persons with depression will improve if not recover, while those with dementia will not improve and may worsen. Waiting is expensive; it may mean months of suffering from a treatable illness. Some depressives just do not recover spontaneously—the disease can go on for years without much change.

Although competent physicians can separate depressions from dementias, they rely on descriptions of the course of the illness and the history. In the case of dementia or depression, relatives will have to supply much of this history. In Table 3.1 are the features that we believe are most useful in making the necessary distinctions. The list is by no means exhaustive, but it does include the signs likely to be most noticeable by family members.

A major distinction, as you can see, is the daily rhythm seen in depression as compared to dementia. In depression, the morning will usually be the worst. Spirits and energy tend to improve as the day wears on. This is by no means always pronounced, and it may not be observable at all, but at least the opposite pattern is extremely rare in our experience. In contrast, dementia worsens notably with increasing fatigue and therefore is most apparent toward the end of the day. Another feature worth noting is the tendency of depressed persons, especially elderly persons, to attempt to medicate themselves with alcohol and drugs. In dementia, drug use seems to decline. Even alcoholics undergoing a dementing process tend to reduce their intake. This tendency is pronounced enough that increased use of alcohol or drugs points strongly to depression as the first diagnosis.

## VASCULAR DISEASE

Vascular disease, often called *arteriosclerosis* or *hardening of the arteries,* affects the arteries which bring blood to the brain. Until the last two decades, this disease was regarded as the cause of nearly

***Table 3.1 Signs and Symptoms Distinguishing Depression from Dementia***

| DEPRESSION | DEMENTIA |
|---|---|
| Uneven progression over weeks | Even progression over months or years |
| Complains of memory loss | Attempts to hide memory loss |
| Often worse in morning, better as day goes on | Worse later in day or when fatigued |
| Aware of, exaggerates disability | Unaware of or minimizes disability |
| May abuse alcohol or other drugs | Rarely abuses drugs |

all dementia. We now know that this view was incorrect and estimates of the frequency of dementia due to vascular disease have since been steadily decreasing. Still, perhaps 10–15 percent of dementias that take a course resembling Harry's will be due to blood vessel disease. Moreover, vascular disease often can be successfully treated, so it is extremely important to recognize its presence and give appropriate weight to its role.

One form of vascular disease is an interruption of the blood supply to the brain. The effects resemble those of DAT and the other dementias. The brain, which uses a large proportion of the oxygen and sugar available to the body, is extremely sensitive to shortage or absence of these vital nutrients. Blood carries nutrients to the brain. Brain cells in a middle-aged person can survive only a minute or two without oxygen and just slightly longer without glucose, the form of sugar most efficiently used by the brain. A stroke is an interruption in the blood supply which continues long enough to produce damage to the brain.

Severity varies. Much depends on the size of the blood vessel which is affected. Blockage of a large artery carrying blood to a correspondingly large area of the brain can produce massive damage. Such a severe stroke could hardly be confused with a primary dementia. In addition to intellectual functions, voluntary movements and other functions such as speech would be affected. Because an artery generally fails over a short period of time, the onset of disability will be abrupt, not gradual as in primary dementias. Also, because arteries are usually paired, with each member of the pair supplying one side of the body, damage will usually be confined to one side of the body. Obviously, paralysis of part of one side of the body and impairment of speech or consciousness indicates a stroke, not dementia. However, sometimes the damage is confined to very small arteries. If so, there may be no observable effect on movement or intellectual functioning from any one stroke. But if several occur over time, and they are scattered among several small arteries, dementia may develop gradually and become the major observable sign of an impaired brain. Most often the disability will progress in a series of small steps corresponding to the blockage of another artery and there will then be evident recovery. Brain tissue can recover from the damage produced by strokes, but it apparently does not recover from the damage produced by the primary dementias. Jerky progression, featuring abrupt worsening followed by gradual partial recovery, is characteristic of vascular disease. However, this idealized course may be hard to recognize in the practical world. Sometimes, the course of vascular disease may be hard to distinguish from that of dementing illness.

Recognition of dementia secondary to vascular disease is important because treatable diseases may be at fault, such as high blood pressure, diabetes, and certain rare inflammations of arteries. Measurements of blood pressure and blood sugar should be part of any routine medical checkup and are essential in any investigation of dementia. Inflammation of arteries will usually produce other effects, kidney damage for example, but some forms can be confined to the brain. The *erythrocyte sedimentation rate* or *sed rate,* which is a simple, routine laboratory measurement, will generally be elevated if one of the vascular diseases is present.

## OTHER SECONDARY DEMENTIAS

Many medical problems besides depression and vascular disease may also look like primary dementia. Such problems may cloud the diagnostic picture and must be rigorously excluded before final diagnostic conclusions are reached. But, just as important, diseases and conditions unrelated to an existing brain disease may worsen an otherwise inconsequential or mild impairment. In such cases, the appearance of severe dementia may lead to a premature diagnosis of primary dementia. Major disability may be due, rather, to the combination of mild dementia and some other possibly correctable problem.

There are far too many illnesses which may have secondary effects on mental functioning to discuss each one separately. Happily, there are general principles which make explanations manageable and simplify understanding.

The brain is probably best viewed as several highly coordinated organs. Though it is more complex than other organs, such as the liver or kidney, it is an organ nevertheless. Therefore, the condition and functioning of the brain is affected by the condition of the rest of the body. For example, infections anywhere in the body may produce toxins (poisons) which have effects on all other parts of the body including the brain. We all have had viral infections. Our joints may ache, we may feel undue fatigue, and our tempers may be short, because of "colds" or "flu," which seem to affect the whole body. The cold, a disease of the respiratory system, is affecting other organs, including the brain. Ordinarily, this presents no special problem. We accept such infections as unpleasant, though we may complain bitterly and even joke that we would rather be dead. But miserable as we might be, our friends, much less ourselves, could never confuse such an illness with dementia. Yet that confusion can occur when an otherwise innocuous additional stress challenges an already marginal brain.

In normal aging, there is a steady decrease in the functional capacity of all organs, including the brain. Apart from the sort of creakiness which we associate with aging, this decline may not be apparent on day-to-day observation. To be sure, older people may be forgetful; this common condition, called *benign senescent forgetfulness,* is considered normal. But it is a result of a decrease in the reserve capacity of the brain. Of course, we begin life with a most valuable excess capacity in our organ systems. In general, we would hardly miss the loss of one kidney or one gonad or a length of intestine or even a sizable hunk of heart muscle. But when presented with extraordinary demands, the system might then not be capable of a fully effective response. This can happen to the brain when the added demand is no more than a mild case of the flu.

Infections may affect brain function in different ways. Acute infections, such as pneumonia, which feature fever and abrupt dramatic onset, sometimes affect the brain by producing a delirious condition. Those affected are obviously severely ill and they seem at least intermittently to be *out of their head,* unsure where they are or why they are there. Although older persons may become delirious, they are somewhat more likely to develop chronic smoldering infections which begin and progress insidiously and are not obviously doing dramatic damage. Infections of the urinary system (kidney, bladder, prostate gland), the respiratory system (especially chronic bronchitis), and chronic abscesses are especially troublesome. Such afflictions, combined with a brain with little reserve capacity, can produce inattentiveness, failure of concentration, and apathy which interferes with the conduct of life. The results can look frighteningly like dementia. If some degree of primary dementia is present, the associated disability will likely be greatly increased. Discovering the source of chronic infection and eliminating it can be difficult, but it must be done because doing so can result in dramatic improvement in brain function.

Hormone imbalances are also a fairly common contributor to disturbed brain function. The thyroid gland sets the operating level of all body processes. Without sufficient thyroid hormones, all tissues, including the brain, function sluggishly. The result is a generalized slowing which may be difficult to distinguish from dementia. This is the more difficult because the onset of the disability is ordinarily insidious and the progression lacks clearly distinguishing features.

The thyroid gland is controlled by the pituitary gland. Erroneous instruction from the pituitary may cause decreased secretion of thyroid hormones, and can produce effects similar to thyroid insufficiency. The pituitary controls many other hormones as well as the thyroid. Manifestations of pituitary insufficiency are therefore more complex though the overall effect can again be quite similar to dementia.

Drugs present extremely difficult and complex problems to those dealing with brain disease. The use of drugs is very widespread and the age groups subject to dementing illnesses are not exempt—far from it. Drugs influence brain function and nearly always adversely. They can even mimic the effects of a dementing illness. Their usual action, however, is to add to the impairment of a marginal brain, tipping the balance to overt dysfunction. This is a common and most important problem of middle and late adult life. We will take up the most important drugs in pharmacologic groupings. Learning about them will thereby be made much easier. The first group—sedatives, narcotics, stimulants, and hallucinogenics—is subject to overuse and voluntary abuse. The second group consists of drugs which are prescribed usually for some specific therapeutic purpose and are generally not abused, but they still may cause severe problems.

**Sedatives** By far the most important group of drugs for older Americans are the sedatives: alcohol, antianxiety agents such as Valium or Librium, and drugs promoting sleep, such as barbiturates. Two distinct effects may produce important problems—taking the drugs and withdrawing from them.

Sedative drugs produce relaxation and intoxication which most people find enjoyable in their mildest stages, and which they very commonly seek to attain. Alcohol is used daily by many people, often in the form of the "cocktail hour." Moderate and controlled use of alcohol is a ubiquitous part of life for millions of us and nearly always it is a pleasurable and harmless part. Yet there is a darker side. Too much sedative drug produces adverse effects, for example, severe intoxication or drunkenness—again, a familiar feature of life.

The amount of a sedative drug which can be tolerated without producing unpleasant intoxication diminishes slowly with age, because of a combination of age-related impairments. The liver, which disposes of most drugs, cannot do so as efficiently; because there is less body water with increased age, drugs distributed uniformly in all body water will be more concentrated; there are fewer brain cells, so the effects on those remaining may be greater; and so on. Most often, this decreasing tolerance for drugs is not troublesome. People adjust dosages slowly as they age and the reserve capacity of most organs is sufficiently great to prevent manifest problems.

It is a different matter when the brain becomes compromised; then any added challenge may prove calamitous. All sedative drugs effectively interfere with the formation of memory. Thus, a drink or two added to an impaired brain may produce signs of dementia. If, as is often the case, light drinking occurs throughout much of the day, memories may be seriously impaired for long periods. Moreover, the use of several sedative drugs is not uncommon, for example, a dose or two of Valium during the day and a few drinks at night. The effects add up.

The importance of drugs to understanding and coping with dementia cannot be understated. If signs of dementia appear, those concerned should think first of drugs. A knowledgeable doctor will always inquire carefully into drug use and may ask relatives to search the affected person's living quarters and bring in all drugs found. No one should be surprised or offended by such requests, or by a test of urine, blood, or both for traces of drugs. These tests have become extremely efficient. One sample of blood and urine is sufficient to screen for even very small amounts of some dozens of drugs likely to produce problems.

Severe problems may also arise when persons who had been taking sedative drugs stop taking them. Withdrawal may include increasing agitation, perhaps delirium, and even seizures. Withdrawal from sedative drugs can be life-threatening and certainly requires medical supervision. Withdrawal from sedative drugs as a cause of mental problems will be nearly always easily recognized. There are, however, two drugs that produce unusually severe withdrawal symptoms in some persons, even when the dosage has been moderate. These are Doriden (glutethimide) and Placidyl (ethchlorvynol). Both can produce puzzling and long-lasting signs of impaired brain function. Although these signs are usually more like delirium than dementia, the whole picture is a confused one. Distinctions are hard to make, especially if withdrawal is superimposed on a brain already compromised.

**Narcotics** One might think that narcotic drugs such as morphine, codeine, dilaudid, Percodan or synthetic drugs such as Darvon would gravely complicate the signs of dementing illness, if not mimic them precisely. But this is not so. These drugs are, of course, commonly used and abused by persons in the age groups subject to dementia. They produce a dreamy, relaxed state, but while they may impair concentration, there is no significant direct effect on memory. Narcotic drugs are often prescribed for severe pain. In general, their use for this purpose is entirely warranted and harmless.

One effect, long-lasting though indirect, may be important in some cases. Narcotic drugs decrease biologic drives. Users may not eat enough or move about enough. They are likely to become severely constipated, dehydrated (starved of water) and malnourished. The effects of this generalized sluggishness may cause a mildly impaired brain to decompensate. But this is quite unusual, at least in our experience. Withdrawal from narcotic drugs is uncomfortable, but not nearly as severe as withdrawal from sedative drugs. There is also little danger of confusion with dementia.

**Stimulants** Here the danger actually seems to decrease with age. Caffeine is the most commonly used drug in this group. Some persons seem extremely sensitive to the drug and become overly anxious and tremulous when taking it. In our experience, elderly people find the overarousal so disquieting that they voluntarily decrease their intake of coffee. Other stimulant drugs include amphetamine (Dexedrine and Methedrine are typical trade names), cocaine, and related drugs such as Ritalin. These drugs, too, seem to be very rarely abused by elderly people. They are used mainly because they are prescribed by doctors in an attempt to improve mental functioning. Despite all their adverse publicity, there may be a limited place for these drugs in improving the lot of the mildly impaired elderly person. The adverse publicity is mainly a result of the extreme overuse of these drugs by young persons during the drug abuse epidemic of the 1960's. At any age, tolerance is a major problem presented by these drugs. In order to attain the stimulant effect (sometimes a mild euphoria), increasing doses of the drug must be taken. With increasing dosage, toxic effects appear. That danger must be considered. The logical remedy, if these drugs are to be used at all, is to take small doses for only a few days, then stop the drug for a few days and then repeat if necessary. The effect of such small dosages might well be significant improvement in mental efficiency, concentration, and sense of well-being with little risk of abuse. However, stimulant drugs are not effective in treating dementing illness and their use should be avoided by the person with an impaired brain.

**Hallucinogenics** This group includes marijuana and LSD, among several other "street" drugs. At present, we think that very few elderly persons use these drugs but that may be changing with the generations. There is no information about their effects on the mental performance of elderly persons, let alone on dementia. On general pharmacologic grounds, we strongly recommend that these drugs be avoided. Even marijuana, which has a benign reputation and is even reputed to have beneficial effects (none have been proven), impairs brain function and is strongly suspected of having adverse long-term effects on young users. Moreover, "street" marijuana is commonly "laced" with other hallucinogenic drugs—currently phencyclidine (angel dust) is often used, but fashions change. These other drugs are capable of producing severe and lasting detrimental effects.

Other drugs taken by elderly persons are unlikely to be taken by choice; they are usually prescribed. Unfortunately, it is the exceptional drug that is not known to cause impairment of brain function in some circumstances either directly or indirectly. Describing all of these drugs would be impractical and would contribute little usable information. In general, the most frequent offenders are these: antidepressant drugs such as Tofranil and Elavil, drugs to lower blood pressure, drugs which calm or sedate the bowel, and drugs used for Parkinson's disease. The best rule is this: Suspect any drug being taken of having an effect on brain function. Be ever suspicious of pills.

# CHAPTER 4

# DOCTORS: WHAT THEY DO AND HOW THEY CAN HELP

Those who must cope with dementing illness will likely meet several specialists in medical practice, each with a particular expertise. These professionals will all be highly trained and most will be fully competent. Understanding what these doctors do and how they go about doing it will give you a much better idea of what to expect from doctors and from the disease being coped with. With this knowledge, you will be better able to plan, and also able to recognize superficial or incompetent medical practice should you encounter it.

Imagine yourself in the place of Harry's family doctor at the time his wife first sought medical advice. First you set about defining the problem. You listen to the account of the events that brought Harry to you and pick out the main problem—the loss of memory. You ask questions aimed at defining the precise sort of memory loss (recent memory); the duration of the loss (several weeks, at least); the type of onset and progression (insidious and gradual). While doing this, you mentally compile a list of all of the diseases and processes which might produce the patterns your questions are defining. Your list eventually includes most of the conditions discussed in Chapters 2 and 3.

For example, you wonder "Was the brain injured?" So you might ask, "Was there an accident? unconsciousness? paralysis?" and so on, until injury is made unlikely. You inquire about alcohol and other drugs and ask Harry about depression: "How have your spirits been?" "Have you felt you would just as soon be dead?" "Have you thought of suicide?" "Has your weight changed?" In this way, you seek to eliminate possible causes, and would begin to focus on the diagnoses which are most likely. However, at this stage, any possible diagnosis, no matter how unlikely it may seem, warrants at least partial consideration. Given a serious and difficult problem such as Harry's, many diagnoses will remain possible even after the most expert and searching questions.

Sooner or later the doctor will probably decide that a complete examination is needed and will proceed to ask questions which systematically explore for symptoms of disordered function in every organ of the body. Headaches? . . . Blurred vision? . . . Joint pains? . . . Constipation? . . . and so on through several dozen questions. A positive response to any of these questions leads to additional questions to probe further the system being reviewed. This procedure is known in medicine as the *review of symptoms.* The doctor will then do a complete physical examination in which he will pay particular attention for signs of disease of the brain or nerves. Finally, several laboratory examinations will screen for illnesses such as anemia, cancers of different kinds, syphilis, and thyroid and other endocrine diseases. Such illnesses may produce mental impairment, and they will probably be caught in the net of an examination by a competent physician backed by a clinical laboratory.

We will not describe here the several laboratory tests which might be used. However, in Appendix A the component parts of a comprehensive set of laboratory tests useful in suspected dementing illness are listed and briefly described. A positive result on one or another of the listed tests, physical findings, or historical information might send the investigation off in other directions. But the listed tests would be the usual components of a standard complete screening investigation.

A thorough examination can detect almost every instance of the diseases described in Chapter 3 which can closely resemble a primary dementia. But the almost remains a problem. Though the undetected case of treatable illness is rare, the consequence of not discovering it is extremely severe. Moreover, even after many possible diagnoses are eliminated, the doctor may still not have evidence proving that a specific illness is in fact present and causing the problem. So the doctor will probably do more elaborate diagnostic testing and ask consulting specialists to conduct other examinations and give their opinions.

Perhaps getting to this point through the process just described sounds as if it were routine practice which should proceed quickly and smoothly. But in the imperfect world in which we all operate, physicians, being fallible, are likely to proceed hesitatingly. Like all of us, they are sometimes victims of false starts and blind alleys. Most often, events move along at about the pace we observed in Harry's case.

Complex and difficult problems invite specialization. The specialists in medicine likely to be concerned with dementing illness are these:

1. **Neurologist:** A physician who deals mainly with diseases of the brain or nervous system, especially those which affect movement or consciousness. A neurologist or a psychiatrist will generally be the primary physician in a case of dementia. These specialists acquire the most experience in investigating suspected dementing illness and they usually provide ongoing medical care for those afflicted.
2. **Psychiatrist:** A physician who is especially concerned with diseases of the brain which produce disturbances in thinking or mood. The psychiatrist also is concerned with problematic behavior which may not be associated with diseases of the brain.
3. **Radiologist:** A physician who uses radiation to diagnose or treat illness. In dementia, diagnosis is the only concern of the radiologist and today, the diagnostic procedures consist mainly of X ray examinations. X ray technology has become much more powerful and complex in the past decade, thereby greatly augmenting the role of the radiologist. Moreover, dramatic breakthroughs in the use of isotopes, which we will later describe briefly, seem imminent.

**4. Pathologist:** A physician who examines tissue to establish diagnoses. Pathologists also oversee most laboratory examinations of blood and other fluids. At an autopsy, the pathologist makes the final diagnosis. Neuropathologists specialize in the examination of tissue from the nervous system. A neuropathologist involved in a case of dementing illness will probably never see the living patient, but only the neuropathologist is qualified to establish the definitive diagnosis.

To this listing should be added two nonmedically trained professionals who are especially important in dealing with dementia.

**5. Psychologist:** Psychologists are most important in the diagnostic effort. They administer and interpret psychological tests which provide essential diagnostic information about brain function. Confirmation that a dementing illness is or is not present is often provided by psychological tests.

**6. Social worker:** The social worker is the intermediary between patients, families, and the many public and private agencies which may become involved with them. A knowledgeable social worker can be immensely helpful to family members in dozens of practical ways. They are usually attached to the staff of hospitals and often patients who become involved with nursing homes or public agencies are automatically assigned a social worker. If this is not the practice in your area, ask your doctor for a referral.

With the specialists come specialized diagnostic procedures. Almost certainly, those with dementing illnesses and their families will be asked to consent to several examinations, and sometimes that decision is not easy. We will later see that hospitalization and extensive testing can be cruel trials for the dementing person. At the very least, the responsible doctor should have the examinations well organized so that the time spent and the confusion inherent in the process is minimized. Families should assure themselves that this is done.

Remember, doctors seek certainty, and some may go to undue lengths, ordering test after test until they come as close as possible to achieving it. Of course certainty would be most desirable, but at some point, the comfort and well-being of the person undergoing the tests become more important. While most doctors are sensitive to these considerations, every real-life situation has unique aspects and judgment is required. Give the doctor the benefit of any doubts, but at the same time, ask that the doctor be able to provide good understandable reasons for everything asked of the patient.

The following section describes the various tests and procedures often advised and administered when dementia is suspected. These descriptions may be most useful if taken as guides for questioning doctors. No absolute recommendations are possible.

## PSYCHOLOGICAL TESTING

At present, the intellectual deficits of dementia, especially the loss of recent memory, can be most precisely estimated by psychological tests. Indeed, in the earliest stage of the dementing process, formal psychological testing may provide the only possible confirmation of deficits in memory formation. Because loss of recent memory is so characteristic of dementing illness, the tests used mainly test ability to learn new material. Failure to demonstrate memory impairments on psychological tests would be strong evidence against the presence of dementia. As treatments are developed, psychological tests will also likely be used to monitor their effects.

Some patients become extremely anxious when presented with psychological tests. However, a skilled and sensitive psychologist can usually overcome this problem and many patients eventually come to enjoy the testing procedures. In general, psychological testing is harmless. While repeat testing may be onerous because of the time required—often three to four hours—these tests provide useful measures of the progress of an illness. A few samples of test items are in Appendix A. Also, in Appendix A is a scale which we use in roughly assessing the progress of the dementing process over a period of time, on the order of six months. It can be administered in a few minutes and it yields a numerical score.

## THE ELECTROENCEPHALOGRAM (EEG)

Often called the *brain wave test,* the electroencephalogram produces a recording of voltage patterns from the brain. These patterns are measured through electrodes at three or more (often eight) positions on each side of the head. The electrodes are applied to the scalp with a pastelike conductor. The procedure is painless and harmless, although the electrode paste in the hair is a little messy.

The brain characteristically produces a rhythm of 8 to 13 cycles per second from its mid and rearward parts. In the front, the rhythm is generally faster (14 to 22 cycles per second) and the change in voltage is smaller. By using several electrodes, the source of the voltage changes can be located fairly precisely as originating from a specific area of the brain. Normally, the two sides of the brain yield symmetrical recordings. In the dementias, the recordings, while often not perfectly symmetrical, are usually not so very unusual in this respect. Rather, the major change which may be observed in dementia is a change in rhythm. This generally does not occur until quite late in the course of dementing illness. Then the rhythm may slow to less than 8 cycles per second, often to 3 to 5 cycles per second. This change is often most prominent from areas of the brain involved with memory formation.

The value of the electroencephalogram is not in proving a diagnosis of primary dementia, but rather in helping to eliminate other illnesses which may look like primary dementia. For example, if the normal symmetry of the recorded voltage is distorted, especially if the asymmetry is fairly well localized, a tumor or stroke is more likely than dementia.

An electroencephalogram may be ordered by any physician, but usually it is administered and read by a neurologist, or sometimes a psychiatrist. Doctors may want to repeat the test several times through the course of the illness in order to follow its progression. This is entirely reasonable if the test is not overly upsetting. In addition, the electroencephalogram may be needed to investigate seizures if these occur late in the course of the illness.

## CEREBROSPINAL FLUID EXAMINATION

As part of the first stages of investigating a dementing illness, doctors will want to obtain a sample of cerebrospinal fluid. Some tests to eliminate important diseases can be done in no other way. For example, syphilis, a disease that is by no means rare, may be present in the brain and reveal itself in cerebrospinal fluid even though the conventional tests on blood are negative. And there are several other diseases that manifest themselves most clearly in cerebrospinal fluid.

Obtaining cerebrospinal fluid may sound dangerous, but it is actually a routine process which any doctor can perform. The pain and discomfort are quite moderate, hardly more than a needle stick. Because the needle enters the cavity containing the fluid several inches below the ending of the spinal cord itself, there is no possibility of paralysis because of injury to the spine. Indeed, the procedure has only one fairly common side effect—a throbbing headache which may be quite distressing for a few hours. Fortunately, severe headaches not only are rare but can be readily relieved by treatment.

## X RAYS AND THE CAT SCAN

Conventional X ray examinations are of limited value in dementia because they cannot produce an image of the brain itself. They are used instead as a crude screen to catch other pathological processes which might stimulate dementia. However, in recent years, several new techniques have been developed which form images of brain tissue itself. These advances have truly been revolutionary. Their contribution to diagnosis and research has hardly begun to be fully realized. Among these new techniques, the CAT scan is the most important in dementia. The CAT scan can outline the brain, including its surface and its ventricles. Moreover, it can do this in simulated *slices* so the brain can be seen at several levels. For example, an image of the brain may be produced on a horizontal plane (one parallel to the floor) at the level of eyebrows. Figure 4.1 shows two typical such slices.

This amazing technology has replaced several older procedures including one with particular importance in dementia, pneumoencephalography. That procedure, which produced severe side effects, is now happily obsolete. The CAT scan allows us actually to see evidence of multiple small injuries such as several small strokes or tumors, which can produce an outcome much like dementia. It can also discover low pressure hydrocephalus. In these ways the CAT scan is unique and irreplaceable. However, a CAT scan may not provide proof that an early dementia is pres-

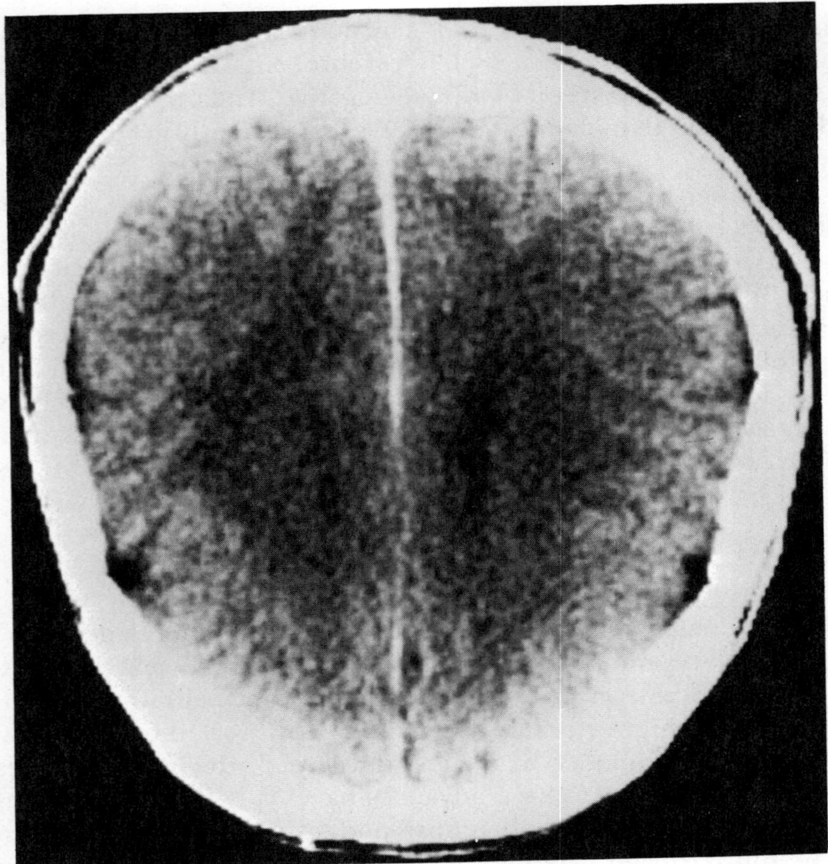

*Figure 4.1a*
Results of CAT scans. The brain above is normal.
Courtesy of Dr. Larry Gold

ent. There is so much overlap between CAT scans from normal persons and those with early dementia that definitive diagnosis is not usually possible. With age, there is some symmetrical shrinkage of the brain even in mentally intact normal persons. Little shrinkage may be present in the early stages of dementia. It is only fairly late in the course of the dementia, that the shrinkage of the brain becomes unmistakable on the CAT scan.

## BRAIN BIOPSY

It is possible surgically to remove a small sample of brain tissue through a hole made in the skull. Then a pathologist can use the

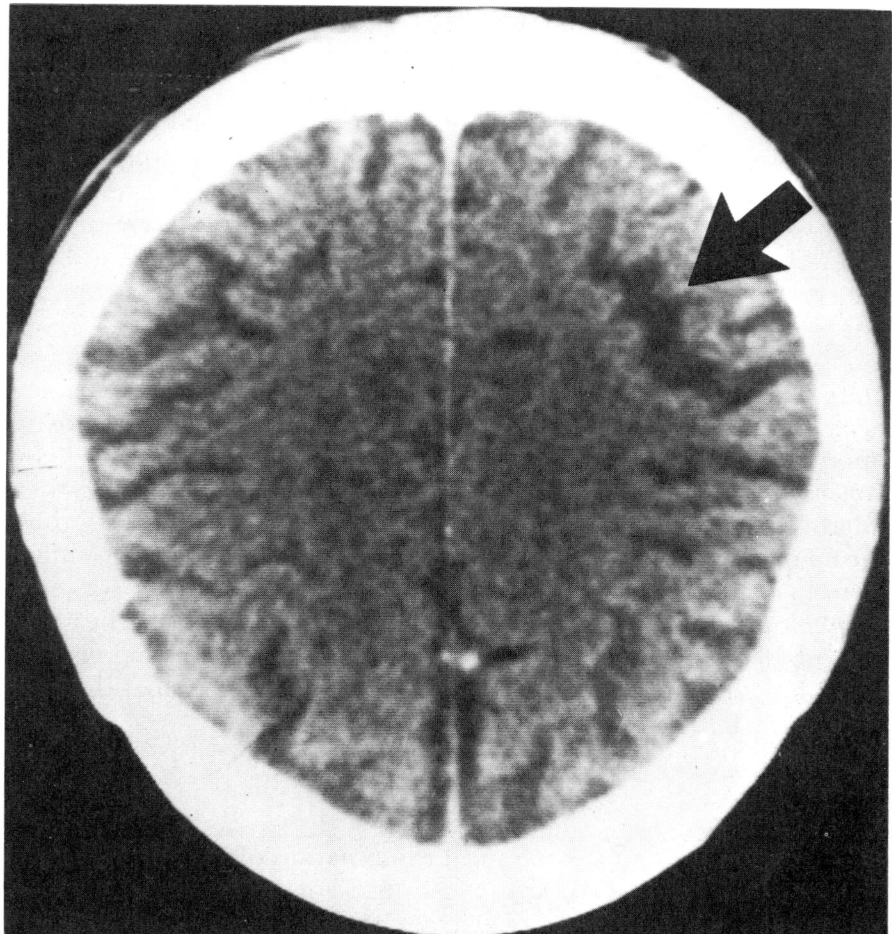

*Figure 4.1b*
The brain above is atrophic. The arrows indicate crevices on the surface of the brain (sulci) which widen because the brain itself shrinks.
Courtesy of Dr. Larry Gold.

tissue to make a definite diagnosis. Obtaining a piece of tissue for diagnostic use is known in medicine as a biopsy. The surgery need not affect brain function in any measurable way because the amount of brain removed is small and it is removed from a silent area, a part of the brain with no discrete function.

Despite its lack of measurable effect on the brain itself, biopsy has little, if any, place in the current management of dementing illness. General anesthesia is necessary and that entails a significant risk. The entry through the skull is not a benign procedure and may produce fairly severe discomfort throughout the postoperative period and into convalescence. These deterrents would matter little if the procedure could make any practical difference in outcome; but it cannot because, in all except the rarest cases, having a correct diagnosis makes little practical difference, as treatment would not be changed. Moreover, early in the course of the illness, the changes in brain tissue are not so widespread that they are certain to appear in a small sample of tissue. Diagnosis might not be possible, even with a biopsy.

In the future, effective treatments for one or more of the primary dementing illnesses may well appear and these may possibly justify the trauma of brain biopsy in order to get an exact diagnosis upon which to base treatment. Hopefully, we will by then have discovered methods of examining tissue more exact than those the microscope provides. But these developments are still in the future. For now, only exceptional circumstances might provide sufficient justification for imposing the risk and discomfort of surgery on persons with dementia. A doctor advising biopsy should be able to explain the need for it to the full satisfaction of family members. In all but the rarest circumstances, pathological examination can wait until the autopsy.

## THE AUTOPSY

The importance of a pathological examination of brain tissue obtained by autopsy (rarely biopsy) cannot be overstated. It is at present the only way that a conclusive diagnosis can be established, and is likely to remain so, far into the future. Without an examination of brain tissue, the best diagnosis made is still only a clinical opinion, and that is just not reliable enough for most serious purposes.

Autopsy is often difficult to contemplate or discuss. To the professional, the autopsy is no more than surgery performed after death. There is no disfigurement or disrespect; tissue is removed for examination and that is all. But nonprofessionals do not have that background of experience and, especially when recently bereaved, may not be able to concentrate on dispassionate explanations. Even when the importance of accurate diagnosis is understood, giving permission to obtain it through autopsy may be difficult. Relatives often imagine that disfigurement, disrespectful handling of tissue, and mutilation are likely results. For some, religious beliefs may forbid the procedure. Often relatives feel that the deceased had already suffered enough.

Finally, there is the question, "What good is an autopsy going to do him or her?" The answer of course is "none at all," but, for survivors, having a correct diagnosis is extremely important. The reasons for this have been presented earlier, but because the subject is so important, we will repeat them without apology.

1. As treatments are developed, they will surely be effective only in very specific illnesses. Since anyone who develops a dementing illness will, with overwhelming probability, have the same illness as a similarly affected family member, a presumptive diagnosis can be made quickly and treatment begun. This may save a great deal of time during which brain tissue may be saved from destruction and may prevent trials of ineffective and possibly uncomfortable or dangerous treatment.
2. The various dementing illnesses carry different genetic risks and have different natural histories. Knowing which illness is present and threatening the family will help those concerned to plan realistically.
3. A reason for obtaining autopsies which was not mentioned before is also most important, though of no direct benefit to bereaved families. Brain tissue is essential to many of the research programs most likely to discover the basic biochemical, physiologic and pharmacologic properties of the progressive dementias. Remember that no animal develops the neuropathology of DAT and it is hard to say that an animal can really develop dementia. Human tissue is critically needed. We will later give advice on how to judge the merit of medical research projects.

The questions we have most often been asked about autopsies are these:

1. **Who can give permission for an autopsy?** In order of their legal standing, the following relatives can give permission: spouse, adult son or daughter, parent, and adult sibling. Among relatives, the one with the highest legal standing who is available and competent must agree. That is, a spouse, if living and competent, must agree and if the spouse does not, no other relative

or combination of relatives can override that decision. A legally appointed guardian or a judge having jurisdiction can order an autopsy.

2. **To whom should the permission be given?** In nearly all cases, the physician who last attended the deceased will be in position to see to the autopsy. Other helpers are the Alzheimer's Disease and Related Disorders Association (which we will refer to often using the abbreviation ADRDA), a local medical association, or a local pathologist. However, only a neuropathologist is really qualified to examine brain tissue. ADRDA has compiled a directory covering North America of qualified pathologists, contact persons, and research projects which need tissue. Appendix B contains a complete listing of ADRDA chapters with addresses and telephone numbers. There are similar lay organizations concerned with Huntington's disease and hereditary ataxias which, although not strictly dementias, are nevertheless a related group of brain diseases. Appendix B also lists contacts for those organizations.
3. **Can we have an open casket if an autopsy is done?** Of course. There is no disfigurement at all. The only visible sign is a cut in the skin at the back of the neck and that can only be seen on close examination.
4. **Can we learn what was found?** Yes. It takes about six weeks to process tissue, examine it, and prepare a report. That report will be available to immediate relatives and most doctors will be glad to explain it in detail.
5. **Should the entire body be studied?** In general, yes, especially if there is any doubt about the cause of death. However, only brain tissue is needed to establish a specific diagnosis from among the progressive dementias.

Those are the major considerations. Together with conscience and sensitivity, they are what is needed to reach a sensible decision.

One final point needs to be made regarding doctors. Patients and families should ask themselves constantly: "Are we getting the best available care?" The physician is professionally obligated to provide the best possible care. If he or she has any doubt on this matter, the physician must call for consultants or make a referral to someone better prepared or qualified. In addition, it is always the right of patients and families to choose another doctor. In the practical world, these matters are generally settled by obtaining consultation. Families can always ask for a second opinion from a doctor they choose or accept the recommendation of their current doctor. Any doctor should accept such a request in good grace, and nearly all will. Not doing so should raise questions about the doctor's competence. Do not be hesitant or timid. If in doubt, act.

# CHAPTER 5

# CAUSES OF PRIMARY DEMENTIA: FACT AND FICTION

We do not know what causes primary dementia. Even to speak of a single cause is misleading, because dementia is the result of a complicated sequence of events involving many contributing factors. Medicine has learned well with many painful lessons from chronic illnesses such as arthritis, diabetes or cancer: Simple causes have proven illusory.

In this chapter, we shall take up the factors known or strongly suspected to contribute to dementia. None should be thought of as a cause in itself, but rather as another piece of the puzzle. To the caregiver or relative of someone with a dementing illness, who understandably seeks cause and solution, this description of the limits of our knowledge may be disappointing. But the boundaries of our knowledge are expanding rapidly. Little of the material in this chapter was known ten years ago and much was unknown five years ago.

## GENETIC FACTORS

Genes are the single causal factor convincingly demonstrated to be at work in most dementing illnesses. The only other causal factor generally accepted by scientists is viral infection in Creutzfeldt-Jakob disease. Therefore, some knowledge of the basic principles of genetics will be most helpful. However, the causal chain of events is not simple nor are its major features adequately understood. The action of genes cannot be understood except in relationship to the environment in which they operate. Genes basically respond to moment-to-moment changes in their environment. Moreover, diseases with effects as broad as the dementias surely involve a large proportion of the genes of the body in one way or another. To add further complications, most fairly common diseases, such as DAT, probably have several different forms, each one depending on different genes or combinations of genes.

**Huntington's Disease** Huntington's disease provides the most straightforward introduction to genetic factors in dementia. Inheritance of this disease seems simple because it appears in almost exactly 50 percent of the first-degree relatives (the parents, siblings, and children) of an affected person. First-degree relatives share in common an average of 50 percent of their genes. This 50 percent constitutes a genetic ratio, the one associated with a dominant gene. The explanation of this constant ratio is not forbiddingly complex and the curious can find full explanations in any elementary genetic text. However, an understanding of genetic theory is not central to understanding the place of genetics in dementia. Rather, the complex ecology of this seemingly simple disease does usefully illustrate more general properties of genetics applied to dementia.

One such general property is this: We cannot know from the information now available just how many different diseases appear to us as the single disease, Huntington's disease. We have not yet discovered separate variants of the disease, yet we must strongly suspect that such variants exist. So many examples of splitting one apparent disease into two or three or more have been found that no one with experience in medical genetics would be surprised to learn that Huntington's disease had been likewise teased apart. It is therefore likely that progress in understanding dementing illnesses will proceed stepwise. Each step will mark a discovery involving another one among several variant forms of each disease and a treatment successful in one variant may well not be successful in another. No doubt many examples of such processes will be discovered among the dementias.

Like other progressive dementias, the manifestations of Huntington's disease can vary widely. It can begin in infancy or extreme old age. It may manifest as a fulminating illness or as an indolent, barely progressing one. Usually a peculiar involuntary writhing movement marks the disease, but some cases feature muscular rigidity and, in others, there is no apparent involvement of muscles at all. We know of one case of the latter kind which several very highly regarded physicians had diagnosed as DAT. The autopsy results proving Huntington's disease came as a great surprise. Some persons known to possess the gene have lived into their seventies and eighties without exhibiting signs of the illness. Presumably they would have shown signs eventually, but they just did not live long enough. All of these types of variability must be attributed to genes which modify the action of the gene which causes the disease, or to environmental factors, or to some combination of genes and environment.

Such complications are the general rule in chronic disease. Medicine has long recognized this, but that has not made the diseases any easier to understand. However, change is in the wind. Recent advances in the basic biological sciences have raised the real possibility that the structure of all human genes may become known and that their positions relative to one another may be mapped. Futuristic, yes indeed. Yet describing such possibilities, as we shall do later, is warranted because they belong in the foreground of our expectations.

Huntington's disease also usefully illustrates several general principles which are immediately practical. One such is the effect of age at onset on the probability that a given relative of an affected person will develop the same disease. For example, we know that half of the children of a known case of Huntington's disease will become affected. We also know that the average age at onset of the illness is about forty-six; that is, half of the cases develop before that age and half after. Now, what is the remaining risk to the forty-six-year-old son or daughter of an affected person? It started as 0.5 (or one-half) but now it must be less because some of the risk—forty-six years—has been lived through. But just how much less? This is a most practical question and it comes up again and again in practice. Sadly, the common sense answer is not the correct one. It at first seems that if the initial risk was ½ and that half of the cases would have developed by about age forty-six, then the risk should be reduced by half and become one quarter. This solution neglects the fact that the sibling at risk in our example may have been one of the 50 percent who did not get the gene at birth.

The probabilities are complicated to describe but easy to see. Figure 5.1 is a diagram of the probabilities; 50 percent of the children of Huntington's cases will have the gene. Half of the 50 percent of the children who got the gene at birth, or 25 percent of all the children, will have developed the disease by age forty-six. Of course, the 50 percent of children who did not get the gene will not develop the disease. A little study of Figure 5.1 will demonstrate that those who will develop the disease after age forty-six constitute one third of all of those well at age forty-six. Therefore, the actual remaining risk is 0.33, not 0.25.

Understanding this concept will probably take a little looking at Figure 5.1, and working through example problems, but that

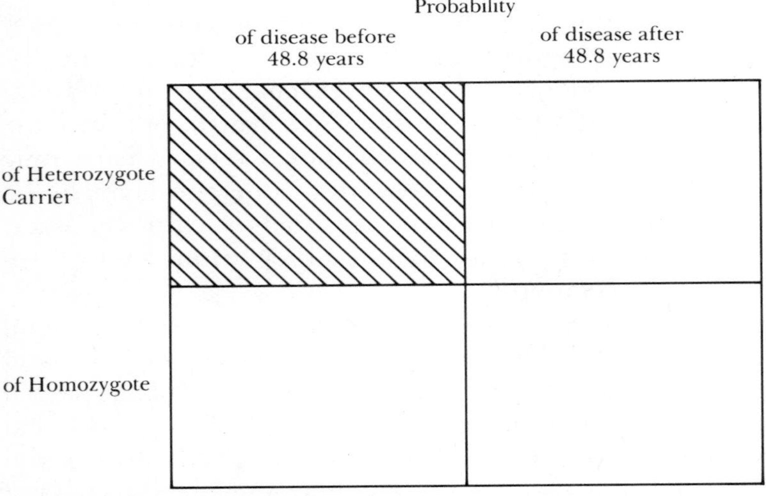


*Figure 5.1*
Diagramatic representation of the remaining risk for Huntington's disease for a first-degree relative of a known case. The square represents the total probability for the newborn child of a person who has the gene for Huntington's disease. Half of such children will have received the gene (the heterozygote carrier). Half of the children are homozygotes and will remain normal. By age 48.6, half of those who have the gene will have developed the disease, corresponding to the cross-hatched area. Of course, the homozygotes, who did not get the gene at birth, had no risk for disease. Those still at risk, represented by the upper right quadrant, constitute one-third of those well at age 48.8. Therefore, the remaining risk for those well at age 48.8 is one-third or 0.33.

understanding is fundamental to understanding genetic risks. The basic data needed are a distribution of observed ages at onset of illness. This is presented in Appendix C for Huntington's disease, Pick's disease and DAT. The algebra needed to use those and similar distributions for other diseases at first may look formidable but it is really quite simple. Appendix C contains the formulas and several worked examples.

**DAT** The genetics of DAT are more difficult than those of Huntington's. Figure 5.2 presents the basic data. The lines in the graph represent cumulative risks at the indicated ages. For example, the risk to siblings up to age seventy-five is about 7 percent. This risk is the sum of the risks to age sixty-five (about 1 percent), between age sixty-six and seventy (about 2.5 percent) and between seventy-one and seventy-five (about 3.5 percent). The lines are reasonably straight, which means that the added risk during each age in-

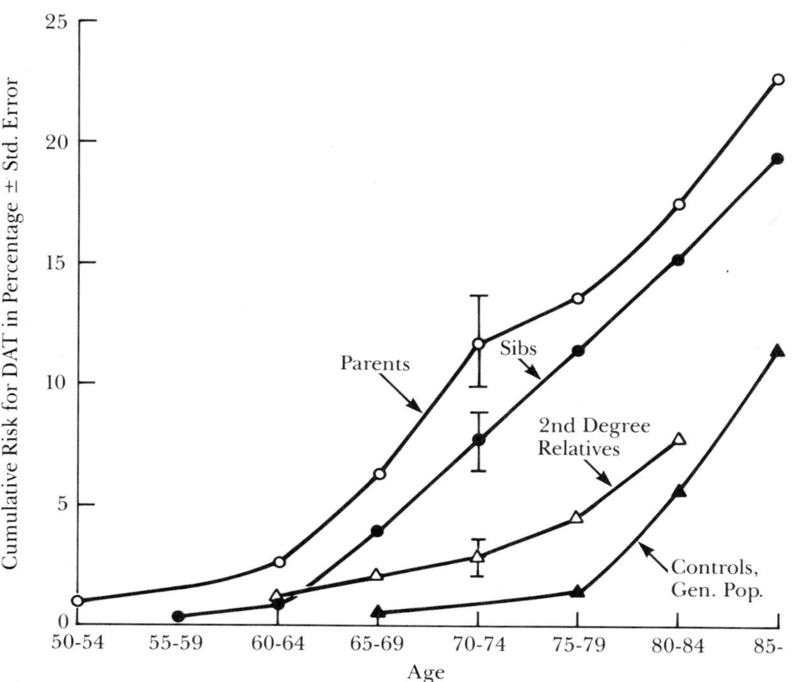


*Figure 5.2*
Cumulative age-specific risk of DAT for parents, siblings, second-degree relatives and the general population.

terval is fairly constant—about 3 to 4 percent. There are no estimates available for children because no families have been studied long enough for children to grow up and become affected. However, children probably have about the same risk as siblings. Second-degree relatives (for example, uncles, aunts, grandchildren) have a considerably reduced risk, as genetic theory predicts, and in practice are found to be affected only in high-risk families, as will be described below.

It is important to underscore that the risks graphed in Figure 5.2 are *age-specific;* they are the risks of becoming affected by any specified age. Usually, only overall percentage risks are cited, for example, 50 percent for a first-degree relative of a Huntington's case. But clearly, in the case of DAT, the impact of a given risk is much different if it applies to age fifty or age eighty. When data are available, age-specific risks are much more informative than overall risks.

As depicted by the far right line on Figure 5.2, at older ages, DAT begins to occur among members of the general population and will eventually affect some 20 to 30 percent of those of us who live long enough. Viewed from this perspective, the main effect of having a first-degree relative with DAT is a risk of developing the disease earlier in life than would someone without such a relative. This difference in age can be roughly estimated from Figure 5.2. If a ruler is placed parallel to the $x$-axis of the graph (the $x$-axis is its bottom line) at the 5 percent point of the $y$-axis, it crosses the sibling line at about age seventy-two and the general population line at about age eighty-five, a difference of thirteen years.

The risks in Figure 5.2 are not really large compared to many others inherent in life. Most relatives of a person with DAT can simply ignore them as being of no real significance. However, some families do have appreciably greater risks. These are families with relatively severe disease, and among the most straightforward ways of identifying such families are age at onset and proportion of relatives affected. Early onset suggests increased severity, and the larger the proportion of relatives affected, the greater the severity. Parents are most convenient to use to estimate the proportion of relatives affected because everyone has only two biological parents, but variable numbers of siblings and children. Also, parents are always older and have therefore been exposed to any of the age-related risks experienced by any other first-degree relative.

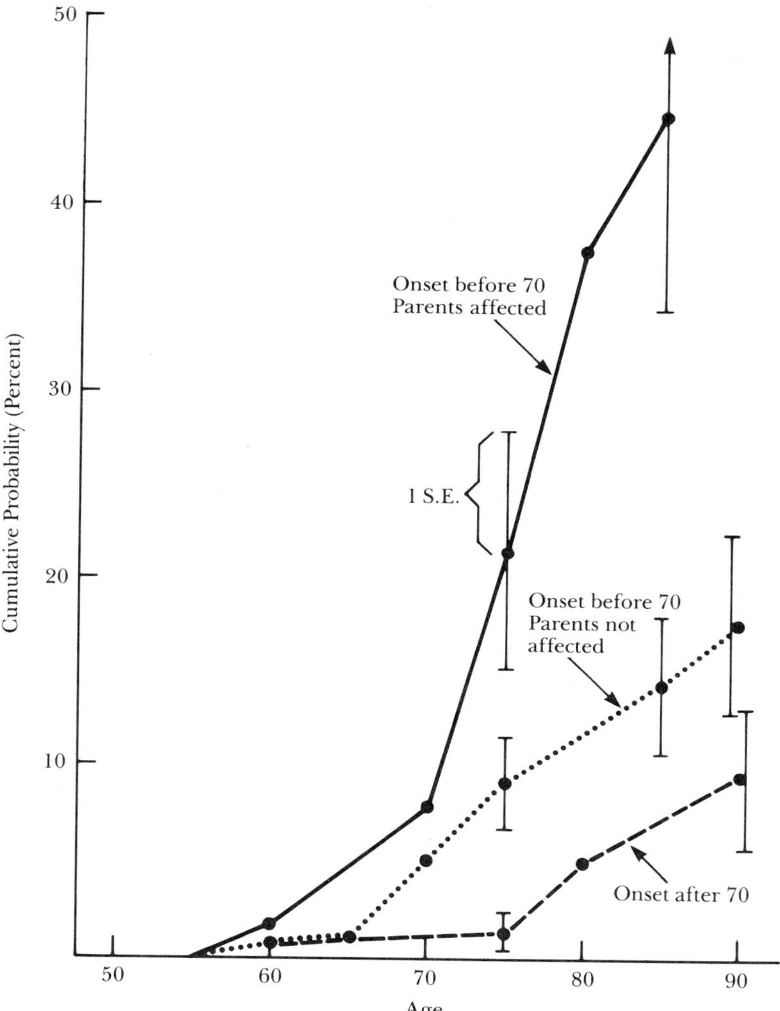


*Figure 5.3*
Cumulative age-specific risks to siblings of probands, with onset before or after age seventy and who had or had not an affected parent.

In Figure 5.3, you can see the risks to the siblings of persons with DAT whose illness began either before age seventy or after age seventy, and whose parent was or was not affected. Again, children have not been investigated and the risks to siblings in Figure 5.3 are probably the best available estimates of their risks. The risks to relatives of a DAT case whose onset was at age seventy years or older is hardly different from the risk to members of the general population (compare with Figure 5.2). The magnitude of the risk increases for relatives of persons where the onset was before age seventy, and for those who had an affected parent. For persons who had both a relative with onset before seventy and an affected parent, the risk becomes much more substantial, reaching 45 percent by age seventy. Happily, there are few such families; many more families at risk are in the lowest risk groups, and two thirds of all families with one affected person do not have another affected person.

However, the fact that some families at genetic risk escape entirely is really just a matter of good luck. Their good fortune has a basis in simple probability, and some insights may be developed if we explain why this occurs. If the true risk for development of illness is, say, 20 percent (or one chance in five), then some families at that risk would escape completely. To grasp this, imagine the probabilities for a family with four children. For each birth, we draw a marble out of an urn containing one red marble and four white ones, with the red marble designating one destined to develop the disease. Then the probability of getting four white marbles in four draws, corresponding to zero affected, is 41 percent; of one affected is also 41 percent; of two affected, 15 percent; of three affected, 3 percent; four affected, 0.1 percent (approximate because of rounding). Similar calculations can be made for families of any size. Thus 41 percent of the genetically at-risk sibships of four would never be recognized because no member developed the disease. But even when allowance is made for such unrecognized families, there remain cases of DAT for which there is no apparent genetic transmission.

Studies of families in which DAT occurs have discovered some evidence that they may contain excessive numbers of persons with Down's syndrome and with certain blood cancers—lymphocytic leukemia and lymphomas. Remembering that Down's patients who live long enough develop DAT, and adding that to the knowledge that Down's patients are especially likely to develop leukemia, seems to provide hints of some sort of complex system of diseases based on a common genetic fault. However, the relationships involved are mainly statistical. To be regarded as established, all would have to be independently verified on large numbers of subjects. Moreover, the risks involved, if verified, would be detectable only in large populations. From the viewpoint of the families concerned, the added risks would be minute and of no practical importance.

**Pick's Disease** Pick's disease is rarer than Huntington's and much rarer than DAT. It is important to note that Pick's and DAT occur in different age ranges. As we have seen, DAT may, in extremely rare cases, begin in the third decade of life. By the fifth decade, it is still a rare disease but then its frequency increases steadily throughout the remaining human life span until 20 to 30 percent of the population surviving to very old age may develop it.

Huntington's and Pick's diseases exhibit quite different patterns. Instead of increasing steadily, both of these diseases rise to a peak frequency in the middle years of life and then decrease. Their distributions are symmetrical around means. These relationships are illustrated in Figure 5.4.

Pick's may begin as early as DAT but it increases more rapidly through about age fifty-four. Even at maximum frequency, it remains a rare disease. Then it decreases in frequency so that new

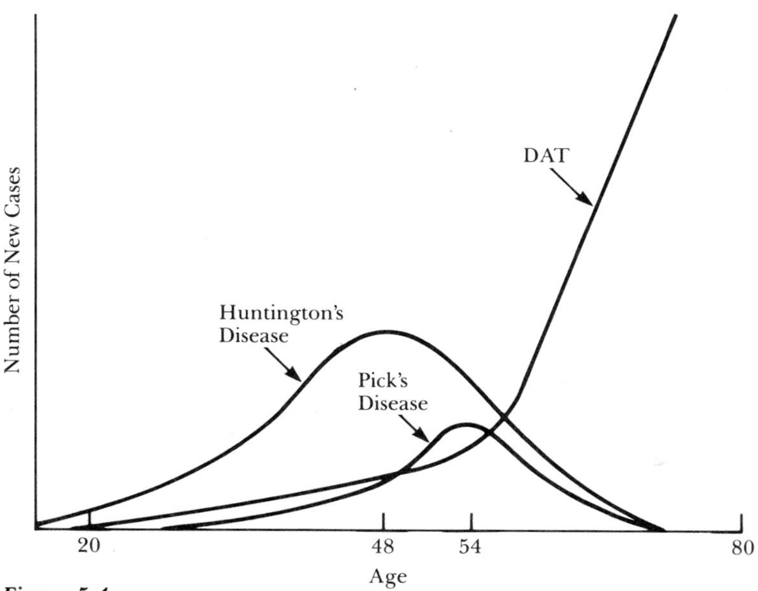


*Figure 5.4*
Schematic distribution of age at onset of DAT, Huntington's disease and Pick's disease.

cases beginning at age seventy-five are extremely rare. The average survival after onset is seven to eight years, about the same as DAT cases with onsets in the same age ranges, and it is likely that early onset again marks a shorter course and greater severity.

The risk to relatives is not nearly so well defined for Pick's as for DAT. Based on just a few families, risks of 25 percent for parents and 20 percent for siblings seem reasonable estimates. These risks are for lifetimes. Not enough data is available to cite risks by the time specific ages are attained as was done for DAT. However, the age-specific risk is not so important in Pick's because most cases begin within a few years of the average age at onset. No risk for children has been directly determined and again, the risk for siblings would be the best approximation.

At present, genetic factors are the only known risk factor for most primary dementias. However, several other possible contributors are strong suspects and, as described earlier, genetics cannot be a complete or sufficient explanation. Now we turn to those other factors.

## NEUROTRANSMITTERS

Faulty communication among nerve cells has been implicated recently as contributing to dementing illness. This communication is accomplished through chemicals called neurotransmitters. It occurs at specific points (called synapses) on the surfaces of nerve cells (or neurons). At a synapse, two nerve cells are very close to one another but do not touch; there is a gap, the synaptic cleft. A schematic diagram of a synapse can be seen in Figure 5.5. The sending neuron contains neurotransmitters stored in small pockets called vesicles. When the sending neuron transmits, it discharges a neurotransmitter into the synaptic cleft where it affects special proteins, called receptors, in the surface membrane of the receiving neuron. When enough receptors are stimulated, the message is received. Most of the neurotransmitter is reabsorbed by the transmitting neuron to be used again. The transmission of a nervous impulse is completed in milliseconds.

In the whole brain, the summation of these simple events becomes extremely complex. There are many different neurotransmitters, and every one of the billions of nerve cells in the brain is directly or indirectly connected to every other nerve cell. The surfaces of neurons are covered by synapses. A neuron receives

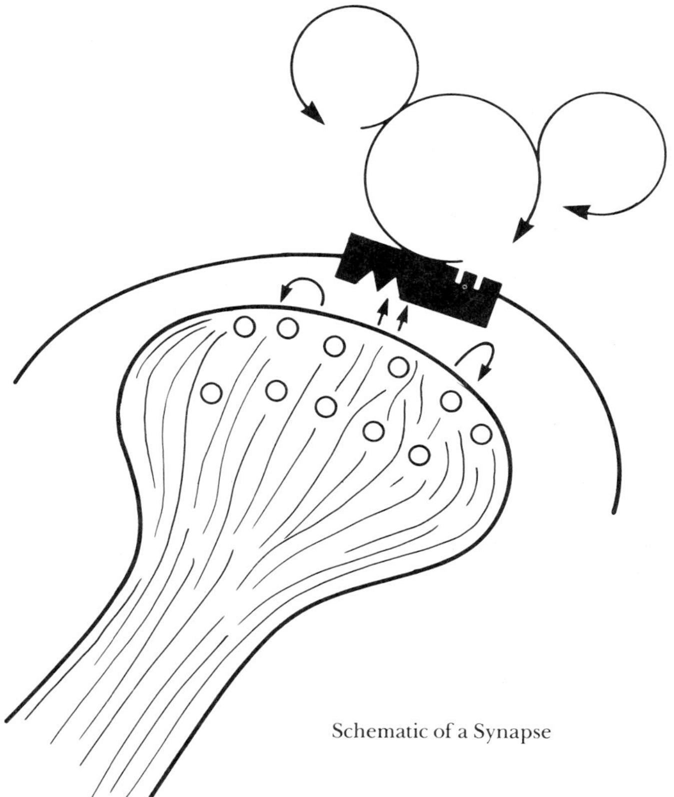


*Figure 5.5*
A synapse. The terminal of the nerve cell in the lower left of the figure stores neurotransmitters in vesicles represented by the circles within the cell. Neurotransmitter is released fitting precisely into a receptor molecule on the receiving cell. The *unlocking* of the receptor facilitates reactions within the receiving neuron. The neurotransmitter is then taken up by the transmitting neuron for later reuse.

messages from dozens, perhaps hundreds, of other neurons, probably using several neurotransmitters. It sends messages to a like number of other neurons. Neurotransmitters can stimulate the receiving neuron, making it more likely to respond, or inhibit it, making its response less likely. Apparently different neurotransmitters are often paired in systems in such a way, that one neurotransmitter may stimulate the system as a whole, while the other neurotransmitter inhibits it.

Neurotransmission is an extremely complex biological system

which has hardly begun to be understood. It is worth remembering that our present rudimentary understanding has developed over the past ten to fifteen years; progress has been extremely rapid. Already, some diseases are coming to be understood in terms of a lack of sufficient neurotransmitter to stimulate the receiving membrane, or a lack of receptors on that membrane. Parkinson's disease is marked by a lack of dopamine, a neurotransmitter at specific nerves. Huntington's disease may be associated with deficiencies in transmissions which require the neurotransmitter gamma amino butyric acid (GABA). Recently, it has become apparent that DAT features a decrease of another neurotransmitter, acetylcholine. One group of neurons using acetylcholine may be selectively dying out in DAT. In the next chapter, these findings will be cited as the basis for some experimental treatments for DAT.

A fault in neurotransmission would most likely have a genetic basis because genes instruct cells how to make proteins. If the instructions are faulty, the protein might not do its job effectively. Neurotransmitters are made by proteins, positioned by proteins, discharged into the synaptic cleft by proteins, and reabsorbed to be stored by proteins. Receptors on the postsynaptic neuron are also proteins. The common thread is genetic relationships.

## VIRUSES

A virus is an extremely small organism, much smaller than a bacterium. It consists of genes and a coating of protein. Typically, when a virus reaches the membrane of a cell, it enters the cell and leaves its protein coat behind. It inserts its genes into the genes of the cell, directing those genes to produce viral genes and proteins. Huge numbers of new viruses are thus produced to go on to infect other cells. The infected cells often die. In many cases, the composition of the membrane of the target cells, which is determined by genes, makes the membrane more or less susceptible to penetration by viruses. In this and other ways, genes affect the likelihood of viral infection.

Most viral infections develop and subside over a short time—the common cold and measles, for example. Some very serious infections of the brain (such as equine encephalitis) are due to viruses, and also tend to have dramatic courses. But some viral infections are quite different. Instead of reproducing itself, the virus may lie dormant in the affected cell for years. Shingles, a common affliction due to the same virus that produces chicken pox, is an example of this process. Some viral infections may even be present at the birth of an organism but may give no sign for decades.

Indeed, the biology of viruses and that of their hosts are most intricately intertwined. Viruses generally infect only one species; human viruses do not infect other animals. Viruses cannot reproduce without their hosts, and they may permanently alter their hosts. Some of our genes, in fact, came originally from infections. The invading genes were taken over by the regulatory machinery of our cells and now we use them to make products useful to ourselves. Much remains to be learned about the place of these parasitic agents in human ecology.

Some "slow" viruses, as those which lie dormant are named, are known to affect the brain, and DAT has been regarded as a possible addition to the list. Presently the list includes

Scrapie, a disease of sheep and goats.

Kuru, a dementing illness limited to certain groups of natives of New Guinea.

Creutzfeldt-Jakob disease, described briefly in Chapter 2.

These infections appear to develop over considerable periods of time—even years—and to progress at a rate much slower than that of most viral infections. They also lack fever or other signs of acute illness, which distinguishes them from other viral illnesses and which makes their natural history difficult to discover. They all produce a dementia which resembles the dementia of DAT.

One peculiarity of the slow viruses—scrapie serves as the prototype—is that they have not been successfully grown in laboratory conditions. Most viruses can be grown in eggs, but not scrapie. Neither can the agent be seen or detected in any direct way. Therefore, the only way to prove that a virus is in fact responsible for one of these illnesses is to actually transmit it. To do this, brain tissue from an infected animal is fed to another animal (often a primate) or injected into its blood or brain. Then years may have to pass before the disease appears. So far, only Creutzfeldt-Jakob and kuru, of the diseases causing conditions which resemble DAT, have been successfully transmitted in this way. However, the hypothesis is an attractive one to investigators, and several animals exposed to tissue from DAT cases are still under observation.

It is possible that a viral contribution to some human dementias may eventually be proven. Because the virus itself cannot be shown to be present unless transmission occurs, the possibility is virtually impossible to disprove. Perhaps infection in an exposed experimental animal would develop if we waited longer, or perhaps the exposure was not effective for some unknown reason. There is always a possible reason for failure. This is a major logical hurdle; a hypothesis that cannot be disproven will always remain possible. Nevertheless, attempts to prove it continue. Investigators are sustained by the analogies to scrapie and Creutzfeldt-Jakob which support the hypothesis of viral transmission. Also, although analogy to syphilis is seldom mentioned in scientific journals, there are striking resemblances between syphilitic infections of the brain and the hypothetical slow virus infections. Syphilis may lie dormant for many years before producing brain disease which often includes features of dementia. Although not due to a virus, syphilis is caused by a peculiar infectious agent, the spirochete, which was extremely difficult to detect through the first decades during which it was sought, and which may still be difficult to detect. Finally, syphilis was once the single most frequent cause of brain disease, a position which DAT may hold today. This is the more notable because it is most difficult for a single genetic mechanism or a single environmental factor such as those we will discuss to produce disease in such a large proportion of the population. But infections do so regularly.

## ALUMINUM

One of the consistent findings in DAT is an excess of aluminum in the brains of human victims of the disease. The excess is extremely small; it can be detected only by using the most sensitive instruments after elaborate preparations. For example, the beakers used in the preparation of the tissue must be special quartz ones. Enough aluminum would leach out of even the highest quality glass to give spurious results. Questions have also been raised about the influence of aging on the concentration of aluminum. Its presence may be common in aged brains and not be limited to DAT. That possibility is being considered in current research projects.

Aluminum is abundant in nature but its biological function, if any, is unknown. Like many other metals, it may participate in one or more chemical reactions as part of an enzyme, but since no such function has been discovered despite intense search, that seems most unlikely. Aluminum does have one specially important property with respect to DAT: It can induce in animals brain lesions that are similar, though not identical, to the neurofibrillary tangles seen in DAT. The difference is important. There are many examples in the history of medicine which tell us unequivocally that in tissue pathology, close is not good enough.

What the minute excess of aluminum in the brains of DAT cases may mean is unclear. It may become concentrated in the remaining brain tissue after the death and disappearance of nerve cells. If so, it would have nothing to do with the disease itself. However, it may remain in tissue samples after destroying nerve cells. Those two possibilities result in directly opposing explanations for the presence of excess aluminum in tissue. Any biologist could devise a dozen more possible explanations and there would be no way to choose among them.

Because aluminum is so abundant in nature, we are constantly exposed to large amounts of it. The concentration of the metal in the tissues of experimental animals can be increased by feeding large amounts of it in the diet, but the source of it in the brain in DAT is unlikely to be a dietary excess. Some fault in the metabolic handling of the metal is much more likely. Practically speaking, the aluminum hypothesis requires that such a fault exist because large numbers of people have been exposed to massive amounts of aluminum in their environments without developing DAT, and DAT victims have not been found to have experienced extraordinary exposures. Therefore, some special vulnerability, most likely genetic, would be required in order to explain the known facts. Certainly there is no reason at all to avoid aluminum cookware or any other source of environmental aluminum.

## IMMUNE SYSTEM DYSFUNCTION

The immune system's function is to destroy or neutralize foreign material in the body. It will destroy bacteria, viruses, foreign tissue of any kind, and even tissue normally present which has been transformed by injury or malignant change. The immune system is a foremost line of defense against disease. However, to do this job successfully, the immune system must recognize normal body tissues and refrain from destroying them. In other words, the system must be regulated; it must know friend from foe. Some diseases are the result of a failure of that very kind—the body attacks its own tissue. The weapons used by the body are specialized proteins called antibodies. These are made by groups of specialized lymphocytes, which are a type of cell normally made in the bone marrow and released into the blood. Other lymphocytes regulate the ones making antibodies. There is some evidence that the functioning of these regulating lymphocytes may be impaired in DAT.

One strong hint that immune system dysfunction may be involved in DAT is the senile plaque itself. It contains a core of the protein *amyloid.* Amyloid is present in tissue in so many immune system disturbances that its presence in DAT at the very site of the injured tissue strongly suggests an immune disorder. Some investigators would substitute "proves" for "strongly suggests" in that statement, and there are other clues. The brain has some degree of ultimate control over the immune system. Neurotransmitters almost certainly are involved in immune responsiveness and therefore an impaired brain could be associated with an impaired immune system and vice versa. In addition, actual antibodies against brain may have been found in the circulating blood of persons with dementia. Such antibodies increase in normal aging, but apparently the excess in dementia is far beyond the usual bounds of normal. This is a difficult area of research and the findings remain equivocal; yet antibrain antibodies do provide a rational explanation for progressive brain damage. They could damage brain tissue by attaching to normal proteins, thus interfering with their biological function and perhaps killing cells including neurons.

The immune system, in all its complexity, is far from being completely understood. Many other possible disorders of its functions apart from the possible presence of antibrain antibodies can be postulated. It is a most logical place to look for dysfunction in DAT and the other progressive dementias.

## HORMONES

A hormone is a chemical messenger secreted by a cell which has a biological effect on other, often very distant, cells. A neurotransmitter is a hormone, albeit a special case because it affects only the cell immediately adjacent to the cell that produced it.

The past decade has seen revolutionary changes in our views of hormones and their place in biology. This is particularly true of the brain. Whole new classes of hormones secreted by brain tissue—the enkephalins—were discovered and are currently being researched. In addition, other hormones have been found to directly influence learning and memory, and their possible place in dementia is being explored. Finally, very recent evidence suggests that other hormonal systems are involved in the regulated growth and maintenance of neurons. No results specifically relevant to DAT or other dementias have so far been discovered, but these areas of inquiry are at the very frontier of research. Since changes in the life cycle—menopause, and aging—are associated with hormonal changes, this is a promising place to look for causal factors in an age-related disease. In the next chapter, some efforts in this direction will be described.

# CHAPTER 6
# THE TREATMENTS

No treatment of the basic disease process has yet been proven effective for any primary dementia. Despite this, the atmosphere in medical research centers is one of expectancy (not that effective treatments will appear this year or next—in ten years, quite possibly; in twenty years, likely). The reasons for this optimism will become more apparent in this chapter. But in addition to supporting a more positive attitude, the same background knowledge will provide a basis for evaluating current attempts to treat the range of problems associated with dementing illness. Just avoiding misguided treatments based on inadequate evidence of fraudulent claims could be a valuable benefit. We begin with current attempts at direct treatment of dementias of the Alzheimer type and Huntington's disease. Later in the chapter we describe the practical management of persons with dementia.

## DEMENTIA OF THE ALZHEIMER TYPE (DAT)

A great impetus to new research in DAT was the demonstration that the activity of the specific enzyme choline acetyl transferase was greatly reduced in brain tissue from DAT victims. An enzyme is a protein which acts as a catalyst for a specific chemical reaction. When active enzyme is present, the chemical reaction which it facilitates proceeds at its biologically efficient rate. If enzyme activity is lacking, the rate will usually be too slow and the reaction may not proceed at all. Choline acetyl transferase is vital to the chemical reaction which combines choline with an acetyl group to produce acetylcholine. Acetylcholine is a neurotransmitter. Remembering from Chapter 5 that communication between nerve cells depends on neurotransmitters, it is reasonable that lack of it would produce serious deficits in brain function. Acetylcholine is used by huge numbers of nerve cells—probably millions—so if communication involving those cells is impaired, mental activity would surely be profoundly crippled.

Enzyme activity is usually measured by the amount of product (acetylcholine in this case) produced over a specified time period. The amount of product can be chemically measured, whereas it is generally not practical to measure the actual amount of enzyme. Therefore, there are several possible explanations if reduced amounts of acetylcholine are being produced by DAT brain tissue:

1. Not enough enzyme may be produced by brain cells although the cells are present in normal numbers.
2. Enough enzyme may be produced but it may be defective and thus not fully efficient.
3. Enough enzyme may be produced and it may be fully effective but there may not be enough raw material (choline or acetyl or both) available to use in making the product.
4. Some cells producing the enzyme may have died for some unknown reason and the remaining cells, though producing enzyme with normal efficiency, cannot make up the loss.
5. Normal amounts of a normal enzyme are produced but the enzyme is being inactivated or destroyed before it can do its work.

These possibilities and others are being or will be tested by research laboratories. Meanwhile, the finding of decreased activity of choline acetyl transferase does suggest logical treatments which are today being tried. These first attempts, though crude, are important. They mainly consist of giving large amounts of choline in the diet. While acetyl is present in ample amounts in brain, choline must be supplied by other tissues or by diet. So if either component of acetylcholine is lacking (possibility 3 above), it probably will be choline. Moreover, if acetyl choline transferase is present in abnormally small amounts, or if its efficiency is somehow compromised (possibility 1 or 2), an extra supply of choline, coupled with the ample amounts of acetyl naturally present, could shift normal equilibrium and force the production of additional acetylcholine. Many metabolic processes behave in this way. The more raw material available, the more product produced, and if the product is lacking due to some disease, forcing the system to make more may lessen the signs and symptoms of the disease. That reasoning led to an effective treatment for Parkinson's disease (with L-dopa, a substance the brain uses to make the neurotransmitter dopamine) and it seems worth trying in DAT.

Given this rationale, two methods of supplying more choline to the brain have received attention. One is to give choline itself as a powder in capsules. The other is to give lecithin, a naturally occurring mixture of fatty substances rich in choline. Either method will deliver choline to the brain, but at this point unknowns and drawbacks begin to appear. Optimal dosage remains undetermined, though it is certainly large, and both choline and lecithin have characteristics that argue for finding a minimal effective dose. Choline in large doses can produce side effects such as nausea, diarrhea, irritability, loss of appetite, and dry mouth. Lecithin produces much the same effects, but its most important negative feature is that it is a mixture of substances, only some of which are converted to choline by the body. In order to get enough choline, about one-third of the total food calories must be taken as lecithin—a most unappetizing and expensive diet. But all of that would be manageable if only we were sure that getting choline to the brain really helped.

Discovering whether or not a treatment in medicine works is extremely difficult. Understanding why this is so troublesome is important, especially for those who must deal with a chronic disease such as DAT. In DAT, one special problem is diagnosis, as described earlier. Because diagnosis is so difficult, treatments have been tried on groups of persons carefully screened so that one can be reasonably sure that nearly all subjects were suffering from one of the primary progressive dementias. However, no specific diagnoses were proven. The subjects may have had DAT or Pick's or whatever. Obviously, assembling a treatment group and later obtaining autopsies to prove diagnoses is extremely difficult; but not doing this exposes the study to the risk that even positive responses to an experimental treatment for DAT (or any other primary dementia) would be diluted and lost because of the mixture of diseases being treated.

Diagnosis is far from the only problem. Another is this: How should improvement due to an experimental treatment be measured? At present in dementia research, this is done mainly by administering psychological tests before and after treatment. A positive outcome is improvement in the test scores, or at least an absence of the worsening scores expected over time in primary dementia. In practice, doing this research is much more difficult than it seems. First, there is a certain amount of error inherent in the test scores. A subject might obtain any score within a limited range just by chance. Also, practice helps, so that the second administration of a test after a period of treatment might produce a falsely high score. Moreover, test scores may be influenced by a large number of factors not related to the disease or its treatment. For example, performance may be influenced by the time of day, by distractions in the environment, the personality of the examiner, minor physical discomfort, mood, etc. Finally, just being given an experimental drug which patients, examiners, medical personnel and all concerned hope will prove effective can boost performance.

Such cautionary notes might seem unnecessarily picky; but medicine has been led astray, not just once, but several times by each of the factors listed above and many others like them. This has led to the adoption of research designs that have become standard for trials of treatment. The basic element is the *placebo control.* Instead of the experimental drug, an inactive substance called a placebo (often a sugar), is given. The placebo capsules or tablets look exactly like those containing the active drug. All concerned should be *blind;* no patient, doctor, nurse, or family member, nor anyone else connected with the treatment team, should know whether a placebo or the experimental drug is being given. One or two persons associated with the project hold that information in coded form until the study is complete and the results are being evaluated. Those persons, however, are not involved at all with treatment, and there are even stronger designs with additional safeguards. One that is commonly used is the *crossover.* A patient–subject is given a drug or placebo for a set period of time and then for a like period is given the drug, if placebo was given before, or vice versa. In all studies of the effectiveness of drugs, patient–subjects should be assigned to the drug or placebo groups on some random basis. Often random numbers are used.

Laypersons should be aware of those principles of research design. The temptation to try something, anything, that just might possibly help a disease such as DAT is extremely strong, and unproven remedies abound. These are nearly always expensive and are sometimes dangerous. Use common sense and the principles of research design described above to reach conclusions as rationally as possible. Relatives will never achieve perfect rationality when trying to cope with diseases having such disastrous consequences and any of us might lean further than is rational in the direction of hope. We must not become so unbalanced as to fall; that helps no one.

Another reason why family members should be well informed about methods of drug trials is that anyone with a dementing illness is likely to be asked to participate in one. Because dementia itself lessens the competency to decide such questions, relatives are often asked to participate in decisions. It is the responsibility of the research team to explain exactly what questions are to be answered by the research project and how those answers are to be obtained. There are a few guidelines to help the layperson gauge the worth of a project. Nearly all projects supported by private foundations or government funds are reviewed by independent scientists in a process known as *peer review* and also by an independent and broadly representative *Human Subjects Committee* charged with insuring that the project meets ethical standards and that any risk to participants is warranted because of potential gain. It is quite proper to inquire about the funding of a project and whether or not a Human Subjects Committee has reviewed it. A project which has passed those reviews is probably scientifically worthwhile and safe to participants. However, many worthwhile projects are not supported by grants. Many of these will, however, have been reviewed by a Human Subjects Committee. In the end, it may be necessary to apply the standards above leavened by good common sense.

If a project seems worthwhile scientifically and reasonably safe, by all means encourage participation in it. It is the only way that progress can be made. This particularly includes participation in placebo-controlled trials of treatment. Remember, no one can know into which group a subject will go, and some subjects will receive only placebos. This is often hard to accept. If there is the slightest chance that a treatment may be successful, no one wants to be the one to prove it by getting worse taking a placebo. Yet there is no other way if anyone at all is to benefit.

Let us now look at how research into choline and lecithin treatment is faring in light of the standards set out above. There have been a few placebo-controlled studies but no crossover studies. By and large, the studies have not demonstrated any benefit from the treatments. However, a few subjects do seem to improve, if only slightly. Picking out a few subjects who seem to improve would be unacceptable in trials of other drugs in other diseases. Nevertheless, these results are regarded as a wisp of hope in DAT research because without treatment there is simply no improvement over time. The disease worsens. So if any improvement at all occurs, even in a small proportion of subjects, just maybe the drug being given should not be discarded. In view of the difficulties in doing research of this kind, perhaps the proper evaluation is that choline and lecithin treatments have not proven to fail. The main import of this is not that these treatments are likely to succeed, but that the theory underlying them may have merit and improved drugs should be sought.

Some of the drugs of current interest which warrant brief descriptions because of the publicity they have received are reviewed in the following:

1. **Deanol:** This drug was once regarded as a most promising treatment for DAT. Like choline and lecithin, it was originally thought to be a precursor of acetylcholine, but that theory of action has been disproven. Its action in the nervous system, if any, is unknown and it is ineffective in DAT.
2. **Physostigmine:** A drug which prolongs the activity of acetylcholine in the synaptic cleft by preventing its destruction. If acetylcholine is needed for memory formation, then physostigmine might improve memory, and it appears to do that at least in normal young persons. It has been tried in DAT, but the results have so far been equivocal. Unfortunately, the drug is so toxic that it can be given only in minute doses and it has a very short duration of action. A major aim of current pharmacological research is to develop a form of the drug which overcomes those drawbacks. Physostigmine can quickly produce death. Do not experiment with this drug.

3. **Aercholine:** The closest preparation now available with the action of physostigmine but which is relatively free of toxic effects. However, aercholine retains unwanted effects that prevent its use for ongoing treatment. It must be administered by injection and it induces nausea and vomiting in most persons. Nevertheless, much active research into possible treatments for DAT is based on aercholine.

Those are the treatments currently discussed with respect to DAT. However, several other approaches have been made to the dementias in general, not targeted specifically at DAT. This is a convenient time to describe those other treatments.

4. **Hydergine:** This preparation is actually a mixture of drugs related to ergot. It is widely used in geriatric populations, especially in Europe. Evaluation of its effectiveness is difficult because Hydergine probably has an elevating effect, though a slight one, on mood. It may possibly have a very slight marginal effect on mental functioning but current thinking holds that this effect, if it exists, is secondary to the effect on mood. If mood brightens even a little, some positive effects on mental function can be expected. That interpretation is consistent with the available evidence.
5. **Neuropeptides:** A group of proteins secreted by the brain and other tissue, which change the operating characteristics of other cells at distant locations. These peptides (a peptide is a short segment of a protein) act in every way as hormones act. For example, one such peptide appears to be secreted in response to pain by one group of neurons, and acts on another group of neurons to diminish the intensity of the organism's experience of pain. It seems like such a neat and efficient method evolved by nature to allow an injured organism to continue functioning in an emergency situation, that it would not be surprising if other peptides modified the operating characteristics of other groups of neurons. Mood is one obvious possibility. Especially intriguing are peptides which appear to exert a tonic effect on neurons that may be essential to the continuing health of nervous tissue. Such essential maintenance functions have been found generally in tissues; for example, weight bearing is required to maintain the calcification of bone, but none has so far been discovered for the brain though their existence can hardly be doubted.

A very recent scientific report described successful treatment of important features of dementia, presumably DAT, with naloxone. This drug prevents opiate drugs, morphine for example, from acting by occupying receptors in brain at which they act; naloxone is a nearly perfect antagonist to morphine. It is thought that the usual occupant of the receptor sites is one of the peptide hormones (an endorphin) described above and that morphine is an effective drug because its physical-chemical properties permit it to lock onto the same receptor. The attempt to treat dementing illness with naloxone amounts to an extremely sophisticated probe of these fundamental biological systems in an effort to assess their place, if any, in these illnesses.

Perspective is needed to evaluate the practical importance of naloxone in the treatment of dementia. First, only seven persons were studied and all diagnoses were made on clinical grounds alone. The improvement was measurable and quite impressive on psychological tests when the scores were averaged. Yet in only three patients was the improvement sufficient to be noticable to family members. How long the improvement lasts and whether further deterioration of mental functions may be prevented or slowed is not known. Second, naloxone must be injected intravenously and it has a very short active life in the body. It is not practical to administer it over any extended period of time. There is, however, an oral form of the drug which has a much longer active life. This preparation will doubtless be given extensive trials. Third, experience suggests caution. As a matter of record, naloxone previously had been reported to produce dramatic improvement in schizophrenia and depression. Repeats of those studies have not produced the same happy outcome. This is not unusual in trials of new active drugs.

Although definitive judgment is not now possible, the preliminary work with naloxone is most interesting from a neuroscience perspective and promising from a clinical perspective. The researchers themselves summed up the situation quite nicely in the concluding paragraph of their report:

> These results indicate that intravenous naloxone may have at least temporary positive effects on cognition in patients with senile dementia of the Alzheimer's type, and the drug may merit further investigations.

Other peptide systems on which experimental work is proceeding have been found to affect memory and learning. ACTH 4–10 is one such peptide. It seems to enhance mental performance, including memory. It is actually a short segment which appears in each of two much longer protein hormones, vasopressin and adrenocorticotropic hormone. This situation appears to be common in biology. During the course of evolution, the genes coding for ancestral proteins were duplicated several times by accident. This duplication provided extra genes which were unneeded for ongoing life processes, and which were thus available for change through mutation. By taking advantage of opportunity, as animals which survive the course of evolution generally do, new hormones apparently were fashioned using the extra genes. The study of such peptides is just beginning. There appear to be literally dozens of them and at least as many suggested functions. So far, only ACTH 4–10 has been actually tested in human populations. It does enhance mental efficiency in normals; it does not appear to benefit primary dementia. Years of laboratory research will be needed before these hormone systems are well understood. But the reward may be very great indeed.

That exhausts the list of treatments and possible treatments of current scientific interest. It is not possible to list all of the treatments which have been advocated or actually tried and found to be useless. Some which have received some publicity in the past are *procaine* by injection, *metrazol, low cholesterol* or *low fat diets, papaverine,* and *anticoagulants* to thin the blood and prevent clots from forming. Two other more recent treatments should be mentioned, *hyperbaric oxygen* and *massive doses of vitamins.* Oxygen at high pressure was reported dramatically effective in restoring brain function. However, this claim has been decisively disproven. Vitamins have been advocated by enthusiastic partisans for virtually all brain diseases, including progressive dementia. There is a definite place for vitamin therapy in secondary dementias, some of which are associated with nutritional deficiencies. Physicians are generally aware of this possibility and order tests which can establish whether or not deficiencies exist. If there is no deficiency, added vitamins are quite useless—they are also harmless unless taken in enormous amounts.

Finally, two very recent entries in the list of proposed treatments should be mentioned. Both have been widely advertised. This is known as *corticosuppression treatment* and is based on the assumption that adrenocorticotropic hormones are produced in excess in DAT. The advertisements we have seen are quite disarming. It is made clear that there is no evidence whatsoever supporting this theory of DAT or suggesting that the proposed treatment might be of benefit. Nevertheless, the treatment is advocated. It would appear that lawyers had done a skillful job. We heartily endorse the disclaimers. Neither the theory of DAT advanced or the proposed treatment is supported by the slightest scintilla of evidence. Another is known as *chelation therapy* and the same evaluation is warranted.

Huntington's disease is the only other progressive dementia for which a rationale for treatment has been developed. In brain tissue from victims of the disease, a deficiency of gamma aminobutyric acid (GABA), also a neurotransmitter, has been demonstrated. And again, the enzyme making it, glutamic acid decarboxylase, is deficient. Based on those facts, some drugs have been given reasonably sophisticated trials. Musciniol, which might directly substitute for GABA, was found to be ineffective. So was Depakine, which slows the normal breakdown of GABA. However, isoniazid, which has been found to increase the concentration of GABA (though just how this occurs is unknown), did at least arrest the progress of the disease in one notable case.

While direct treatment of the dementing process is not yet proven effective in Huntington's disease, the severity of the movement disorder, which itself is quite disabling, can be helped quite a lot. The drugs which best accomplish this are phenothiazines or tranquilizers. These drugs act by blocking the receptors for the neurotransmitter dopamine. It is thought that nerve cells activated by dopamine and GABA respectively have opposite effects. Thus, a deficiency of GABA leaves dopamine to act unopposed; the normal balance is upset and symptoms result. This explanation will probably turn out to be much too simple. But as a hypothesis, it is enormously more sophisticated than anything that could have been suggested a few short years ago.

## MANAGEMENT

Effective and humane management of the person suffering from dementing illness will require all of the practical ingenuity and compassion that can possibly be supplied. No prescription can be written that will cover the specific circumstances of each victim. All we can do is describe principles of management which should allow making the best possible adaptations.

Interactions with a person who has a progressive dementia

must be based on constant awareness of the mental capacity remaining. Guard against overestimation of capacity which is a much more common error than underestimation. In general, be matter-of-fact in conversation. Avoid ambiguity and in particular do not present unnecessary choices or decisions. Say, "Now we must go to the store" and not "Would you like to come to the store with me?" Always be concrete: "Alan is coming to visit after lunch," not "We are going to have company today." Give positive direction: "Now it is time to take a shower," not "Shall we eat now or would you rather take a shower first?" Those general guides may be premature for some families who are having trouble even recognizing that an illness is present. It often takes some time—frustrating, agonizing months—before those in daily contact with a person in the early stages of a progressive dementia grasp what is happening and are ready to begin to adapt to it. Spouses in particular often seem to be unable or unwilling to come to grips with the new realities. For others, directly though not so immediately concerned, grown children for example, the increasing mental impairment often seems more obvious. Disagreements at this stage can be quite painful.

Let us suppose that it is the husband who is developing progressive dementia. His wife does not seem to comprehend the change or offers inadequate explanations of it: "After all, we are getting older" or "He has just had so much on his mind." However, the children, who are usually in their thirties and forties, do realize that something is wrong. What should they do? First, get medical help as soon as possible. Sometimes the physician can act very effectively as the objective assessor of the factual situation the family confronts. Meanwhile, resist the temptation to directly confront the wife; "Look, Mom, he bought salt for the water softener three times last week." Rather, bring up such an example from time to time to illustrate the developing impairment but don't repeat it and most of all do not insist that the wife acknowledge its import. To develop insights helpful in dealing with the wife in such situations, try to conceptually separate her problem into two broad components. First she has to recognize and adapt to the loss of her husband as a partner in the management of the household. This means that she will have to progressively assume his duties or see that they are effectively delegated. This is the easier part for most families. Tackle it first.

There is good reason why taking over specific functions is relatively easy. When we are confronted with situations that we cannot grasp, we become anxious. And this may start a vicious circle because anxiety itself interferes with effective functioning which leads to more anxiety and even worse functioning and so on. Anxiety is an extremely aversive emotion that we go to great lengths to avoid. And so it is with the dementing person who will also be powerfully motivated to escape anxiety. This simple fact of human experience is a great aid to those attempting to deal with a dementing person. Mental tasks beyond the person's capacity produce anxiety. However, the anxiety is usually attached to specific tasks; avoid generalizing deficits. Be specific and concrete—say to the wife described above, "He can't balance the checkbook so you will have to start doing that." Avoid generalizing the situation: "You will have to start managing the money."

The second and far more difficult aspect of the problem for the wife is acceptance of the progressive disintegration of personality of the man with whom she has lived much of her life. She will have to recognize eventually that he is no longer the person he was and never again will be. This is by far the harder part and for most spouses, that realization takes time and cannot be rushed by confrontation.

Avoidance of anxiety generally makes it reasonably easy to get the dementing person to yield control of tasks such as balancing the checkbook and it helps solve other problems. One such problem is the decision to quit work, which will often be made by the victim because work provokes anxiety. Unless the work is intrinsically dangerous—for example, mixing chemicals or flying—it is usually safe to rely on increasing anxiety to time the withdrawal from it.

One frequent exception to this general rule that often proves especially troublesome is driving. In our experience, people tend not to become anxious about driving and continue far too long. Obviously, this is an area where forceful action may be required of relatives. Physicians can be helpful in this respect because in many states, they can file a simple report that will cause suspension of driving licenses.

In the early stages of a dementing process, which in many ways is the most difficult stage, it may seem natural to apply a bit of traditional wisdom which goes counter to what we have so far advised and which we regard as most unhelpful. The basic tenet is that the brain should be exercised as muscles are; "keep the brain active in order to keep it from atrophying." This is wrong. The brain is not like muscle. It will stay active so long as it is healthy. By all means, try to keep ill persons interested in the world around so far as possible and as long as possible. However, being too zealous can lead to overburdening a deteriorating brain with consequent increasing anxiety and decreasing efficiency. Only if a depressed mood is a part of the overall problem is there some reason, though not a very good one, to artificially stimulate interest and activity. Again, the ill person is probably the best available guide. If that person consistently seeks to withdraw from stimulation, don't try to prevent it.

Progressive dementia is accompanied by progressive withdrawal from social activities. The basic ideas outlined above apply with special force here. Dementia makes it difficult and eventually impossible to meet new people or to keep up with social conversation, which is usually oriented to current events. The dementing person will seek to avoid these situations. By all means allow him. Social events limited to few familiar faces, shortened in time, and without distractions such as noise from active children or unfamiliar surroundings are likely to be within tolerable limits and pleasurable to all concerned. However, always err on the conservative side and be alert for signs of anxiety, which provide a reliable signal that respite is needed. These signs are increasing agitation—fidgeting, purposeless movements, expressed desire to leave the situation and, most of all, decreasing mental competence. Be alert for such signs and do not discount them.

Try to maintain a daily routine that features well established landmarks such as regular meals. Make life predictable. Avoid breaks in routine whenever possible and be especially mindful of the total dose of disruption over time. If some degree of disturbed routine is necessary, minimize its intensity. Do not concentrate changes. Instead, extend needed changes over as long a period as possible.

Try to maintain the dementing person in familiar surroundings—the more familiar the better. A change of residence can bring on a disastrous decompensation. If one has lived in the same place for many years, there is a limited amount of new information to be assimilated each day. But in new surroundings, one has to learn where every light switch is located and the simplest geography of the rooms. Probably we have all had the experience of suddenly, perhaps on awakening, being unaware of where we are—and we have found the experience intense by provoking of anxiety for a moment or two. Normally, we recover quickly and no harm is done. But for the demented person there is no such quick recovery. If a move is absolutely required, do it as early in the illness as possible to take advantage of whatever reserves remain or wait as late as possible so that there is minimal awareness of new surroundings. It will always help if as many familiar things as possible are brought along. Keep old familiar furniture and furnishings.

Fatigue is poorly tolerated by dementing persons and it can generally be avoided. Schedule trying activities such as visits to doctors after a period of sleep. Encourage frequent periods of rest, even very frequent. Even an hour of activity may be excessive in some cases and a period of rest may be remarkably restorative. Above all, do not schedule several hours of unbroken activity.

Dementing persons tend to be extremely sensitive to drugs. As we have noted, they will usually progressively restrict their use of such common drugs as alcohol and coffee. If this does not occur, try to limit intake to see if beneficial results follow. In our experience, decreasing the habitual use of drugs may help, but even if it does not, the total intake usually is permanently reduced. Sometimes, usually early in the course of the illness, belligerence or anxiety may become troublesome enough to require treatment with drugs. If so, prescription drugs may be needed and we have found that neuroleptic drugs (tranquilizers) are quite efficient in reducing problem behavior. Usually only very small doses are needed—on the order of 10 to 25 mg of chlorpromazine (Thorazine). However, even small doses often produce side effects in the elderly. If your doctor prescribes these drugs, ask him about side effects, especially extrapyramidal or Parkinsonian effects, and what you should do about them. In fact, narcotics are at least equally effective and do not produce serious side effects; codeine, 15 mg once or twice daily, is usually quite satisfactory, and if tolerance develops, the dose can be increased. The only significant side effect at the usual range of doses is constipation which can become fairly serious. However, such use of narcotics may run counter to federal or state guidelines (not laws) and many physicians will not prescribe narcotics in those circumstances. In our experience, other drugs effective in agitated or anxious states such as diazepam (Valium) are not as useful because they tend to overtranquilize or produce mild intoxications. However, some experimentation may be needed in order to arrive at optimum benefit. Once this happy state is approximated, be oriented toward reducing dosage as the disease progresses.

Earlier we mentioned muscle cramps and generalized seizures as fairly common complications of the later stages of dementing illness. Unfortunately, we have found the conventional treatments for these conditions to be unsatisfactory. We do advise avoiding fatigue for both conditions; cramps in particular seem to be associated with fatigue. We also advise a trial of propranolol (Inderal) for cramps or for tremors which may develop as the illness progresses.

Other common problems include bowels and bladder. Constipation is a very common problem for the elderly, generally. In dementia, this may become especially troublesome because of inattention or medication. Often daily administration of a drug such as Colase will solve the problem. If not, it is probably best to get medical help. Actual loss of control of bowel and bladder can be anticipated in dementia. But that usually comes late in the disease after care at home has become impossible except in homes where twenty-four-hour care and supervision can be provided. However, women, especially those who have had a catheter in place for some reason, sometimes lose bladder control relatively early. A menstrual pad may prove helpful in such cases.

Nocturnal wandering can prove very troublesome especially since others in the home must sleep. Give whatever sedation is needed. Again in our experience, small doses of a narcotic such as codeine are effective. But most often, the phenothiazine or tranquilizing drugs will be prescribed and they are effective and safe overall. Moreover, they have a long duration of action so that an evening dose will be effective through the next day. Give as much drug as needed to sedate. It is hardly possible to give harmful amounts so long as Parkinsonian side effects, if these develop, are controlled by proper treatment. If sedatives are to be used, preventing fluid intake for the three to four hours before bedtime may be a useful precaution against bedwetting or attempts to get to the bathroom while impaired by sedation.

The sexual activity of persons with a dementing illness is not often a major problem. As the disease progresses, interest in sex usually diminishes. Some persons may become hypersexual, but this is rare, though it may appear or reappear at different times during the illness. The best advice is to consult a doctor; a mild sedative will nearly always control the behavior.

In the early stages of the illness, some persons may become preoccupied with sexual concerns and use inappropriate language, which may be entirely alien to the previous personality. Sometimes sexual paranoia may appear. A spouse may be accused of having an affair and mistrust may extend to social conversation. Yet within a short period of time, the same person can become remorseful and cry because of the accusations made. Such mistaken ideas are not held for any length of time and are not of dangerous intensity. Ignore such incidents, try to divert their interest, and generally no harm at all will be done.

Try to give the dementing person every possible break. Doing this entails insuring adequate diet, prompt attention to infections and attention to general hygiene. An apparently small point which may be overlooked is insuring adequate input to the senses. Light can be extremely important. Older persons lose visual acuity, making the surrounding appear dim. A normal brain can largely compensate for this loss by supplying from memory details of the environment which are imperfectly perceived. An impaired brain cannot do this as well and again the familiar vicious circle may be set into play; uncertainty leads to anxiety which leads to increased uncertainty which in turn leads to panic. Unusually intense lighting kept on all night at strategic locations may help prevent this; hallways, stairs and bathrooms are likely candidates in most homes. Usually it will pay to buy and install fluorescent fixtures. The light will be sufficiently intense and can be kept on at all hours at little cost. Unlike incandescent lighting, fluorescent lights use little current when operating. Power is expended when they are first turned on. If they are left on, the bulbs will last for very long periods and the power use is nominal.

Sound is also important. It often helps to have a radio tuned to a station playing old familiar tunes. This is an old remedy, well known to hospitals and nursing staffs. It is worth trying. However, if hearing is impaired, a hearing aid is not often useful in dementia. Apparently the adjustment to an aid, which is often difficult even for normal elderly persons, is nearly impossible in dementia. Also remember that ambiguous communication by sound or distracting noises of uncertain origin are to be strictly avoided.

Sew labels into clothing giving names and addresses in case of wandering off. We have found that conventional measures used in many hospitals to prevent wandering, such as removing shoes or keeping the victim dressed in pajamas, do not help at home. If someone with a little bit of electrical know-how is available, alarms on critical doors can be helpful.

Most of all, human help is needed. Eventually, the dementing person will require supervision for each one of the twenty-four hours in each day. He or she will have to be protected from fire and other hazards, and will have to be toileted, dressed, and fed. Some arrangements to relieve the primary caregiver, usually the spouse, will have to be made. Not much can be done to lessen the problem. Spouses vary greatly in their dedication and resolve, but our experience is that they tend to go it alone far too long. The rest of the family may have to impose the needed help. Act sooner rather than later. Finally, care in a medical facility, usually a nursing home, will be needed. The next chapters will take up that and related subjects.

# CHAPTER 7

# HOSPITALS AND NURSING HOMES

As suggested earlier, dementia often first appears when the routine of everyday living is changed. For example, a family vacation away from home in unfamiliar surroundings may elicit early symptoms of dementing illness. When vacationing, we move from city to city, and sleep and eat in different places. Changes in surroundings and constant movement may be confusing enough for some of us; for the person with dementia, the confusion can be overwhelming.

Because change in environment is a major problem for persons with dementia, their condition often worsens when they are moved into a hospital or other care facility. Besides the change in physical environment, there are changes in personnel, strange noises, constant movement from one place to another to undergo the routine tests which must be done on admission. The demented patient may become confused, disoriented, and lost. This may upset relatives when they visit to find their loved one uncooperative or verbally abusive and more confused than ever, wandering the halls, refusing to eat, shouting, and sometimes behaving violently. Confused persons may harm themselves; for example, they may pull out I.V. tubes. Visits may be stressful. Faced with this, family members may come to believe that they are better able to handle the problems and that their relative with dementia would be better off at home. In a way they are correct—home care should be continued as long as possible.

Indeed, hospitalization of an elderly person for any reason may be quite detrimental with respect to mental status; a heart attack, major surgery and, perhaps most notorious among physicians, a broken hip are examples of catastrophic medical or surgical events which may be associated with abrupt deterioration of mental functioning. The illness or injury with consequent hospitalization most likely acts as a major environmental stress as described in earlier chapters, and as healing progresses, and especially when it is possible to return home, mental status generally improves. But recovery may occur over a very long time and it may not be complete. "He was never the same after the accident" expresses a familiar concept. In such cases, the reserve capacity of the brain may have been exceeded or, in probably more cases than we now recognize, an incipient deficit in mentation contributes to the development of the illness or injury.

However, persons with dementia sometimes need to be hospitalized for diagnostic evaluation or must enter nursing homes for continued care. One instance when hospitalization may be needed, though illegal and immoral in the view of the government and insurance companies, is when the caregiver needs a rest. Caring for persons with a dementing illness is a twenty-four-hour, seven-day-a-week job, and at times this can become overwhelming. While hospitalization may not be the best solution, it may be the only one.

When caring for a demented person becomes intolerably stressful, alternatives must be sought. Most often, placement in a nursing home is the only answer. This decision is often a difficult last resort which many families delay far too long. The caregiver should not make that decision alone; it should be a family decision. At this time, a doctor's recommendation and support for the primary caregiver are important, because the others involved may not understand how difficult the situation has become. To some relatives it may seem that the person with dementia is not "bad" enough for a nursing home, leading to accusation and feelings of guilt. In general, the more the total extended family is involved in sharing the responsibility for such a major decision, the better the primary caregiver and the patient are served. Emotional support is needed, and the support of the whole family can help make the nursing home placement easier for the caregiver.

After placement in a nursing home facility, many families find that the person with dementia is permanently changed. Again, the difference in environment is a factor; however, it is usually due to the progression of the illness. Many patients do adjust satisfactorily, and, although their condition may slowly worsen, they are reasonably happy in their new surroundings. Time helps.

## PSYCHIATRIC HOSPITALS: STATE, VETERANS, AND PRIVATE

### STATE HOSPITALS

To many, the state hospital has a poor image and a bad reputation. Today, state hospitals are trying to overcome that by improving their activities and medical services, and by cooperating with available community services. Though most state hospitals still care for all kinds of patients, many of them are expanding their geriatric care by renovating existing hospital complexes into nursing home facilities.

The better state hospitals have a complete nursing staff and offer many of the same services as a private hospital, including occupational, physical, and recreational therapy. Most state hospitals are self-contained, with laboratories, X ray equipment, and special care units for patients who have physical problems. Social workers and members of the nursing staff are available to work with families. Most staff members are caring people devoted to their patients.

State hospitals are eligible for Medicare benefits, but these benefits are subject to various limitations. The hospitals must be accredited and provide active treatment. Because of the limited coverage in Medicare and private insurance programs, cost for care in a state hospital is assumed by the patient or relatives, if they are able. If not, the state hospital will provide care regardless of ability to pay.

If the patient does have financial resources, he or she generally must pay a portion of the hospital charge. The amount is based on annual gross income and household size. Some state governments bill relatives if the patient can only pay part of the cost. Most state governments structure the matter so that the most relatives will pay is 10 percent or less of the actual average daily cost, which averages between $70.00 and $85.00 a day.

Admission to a state hospital may be by judicial commitment or be voluntary. Information regarding commitment or admission procedures can be obtained from social service departments at county court offices.

Hopefully, the stigma of the state hospital will fade, and families will not be embarrassed or apologetic when a relative enters one. Visit the hospitals. In some states you may find a few badly run, poorly maintained institutions, but you are more likely to be happily surprised with the caring staff and the variety of opportunities for a patient.

## VETERANS HOSPITALS

In 1973, a geriatric research program conceived within the Veterans Administration system was launched. "GRECCs," Geriatric Research, Education and Clinical Centers, were established. The program was aimed at creating centers to develop educational programs and to do research in the aging process and associated diseases.

There are eight GRECC centers. Each center designates a specific area of interest for its study and recruits the needed medical expertise. The study brings researchers and clinicians together to focus on a particular aspect of aging. Some areas of interest being studied are cardiology, neurology, psychiatry, immunology, diabetes and other diseases of metabolism, dementia, and aspects of general medicine concerning the geriatric patient. GRECC centers are located at the following Veterans Administration Medical Centers:

Arkansas
  Little Rock

California
  Los Angeles (Wadsworth)
  Palo Alto
  Sepulveda

Massachusetts
  Bedford
  Boston

Minnesota
  Minneapolis

Missouri
  St. Louis

Washington
  Seattle (American Lake)

In addition to GRECC, the Veterans Administration operates some of the largest health care facilities in the United States. Many are affiliated with university medical schools. All offer a wide range of services to veterans.

Eligible veterans may enter any Veterans Administration Hospital. If special medical advice and treatment is needed, the veteran is transferred to the facility where the needed expertise is available.

For admission into a Veterans Administration Medical Center, contact the Department of Medicine or GRECC.

## PRIVATE HOSPITALS

Private hospitals offer medical care, clinical evaluation, and social service support for families. Most private hospitals do not offer extended nursing care for demented persons—the cost would be prohibitive for all but the most wealthy families.

One private hospital service is the preliminary evaluation. Although this may take only two or three days, patients can easily enter the anxiety–confusion vicious circle in the strange hospital atmosphere. Upon admission it will help to explain the patient's behavior and routine to the nursing staff. Hospital personnel are usually aware of the kinds of problems persons with dementia face. However, some important questions family members should ask are:

Is the patient's room going to be open or locked?

Will eating likes and dislikes be considered?

Is there adequate nursing staff during the night? What diagnostic tests will be done and when?

Families should leave names and telephone numbers where they can be reached if problems arise.

Private hospitals usually have social service departments, which are valuable resources for counseling and information. Social workers help with financial planning and home care planning, and know what services are available in the community. For example, social workers will generally help with rental or purchase of equipment needed for care and with community and personal services, such as visiting nurses, transportation, medical care, insurance coverage, and pensions. Social workers can also assist with placement in a nursing home.

Most social workers know what local nursing home facilities have to offer and will have lists of available vacancies. When it becomes obvious that nursing home care is required, usually family members either have not had time to choose a home or have chosen one and are on a waiting list. Alternative care will be needed. If only minimal care is needed, a convalescent home can suffice over a fairly long interval. Many private hosptials have this type of unit attached. Because of the expense, which averages approximately $4,000 each month, this is not the solution for long-term care.

## SKILLED NURSING HOMES, CONVALESCENT HOMES, RESIDENTIAL HOMES: DIFFERENCES, SIMILARITIES AND WHICH ARE IMPORTANT

### SKILLED NURSING HOMES

Skilled nursing homes provide twenty-four-hour nursing care and also offer rehabilitation services. A home including these kinds of services is the choice for persons who are convalescing or for elderly people who have a long-term illness.

Nursing care is provided by a staff of registered and licensed practical nurses who can administer medications and can implement procedures ordered by physicians. In addition to nursing care, there is an emphasis on physical and occupational therapy. Trained therapists work with doctors to develop specific plans for the individual patient's needs.

A skilled nursing home may be part of a medical complex or it may be a separate facility. It is the most expensive type of home.

If the home has been certified by Medicare* all services for the first twenty days will be paid by Medicare (if the patient needs medical care). After the first twenty days, Medicare will pay a portion of the daily rate for the next eighty days. After that, other arrangements must be made. Unfortunately, persons who have been classified as having dementia are considered only to need custodial care. In order to receive Medicare benefits they have to be classified as "needing medically skilled nursing care."

Because of the limited number of days of hospital or nursing home care for which Medicare will pay, family members should be aware of the restrictions of the *benefit period.* Medicare will pay for care when a new benefit period begins. A benefit period starts the first time the patient enters a hospital after hospital insurance begins. However, when all Medicare days have been used, in order to be eligible for a new benefit period to begin, the patient has to have been out of a hospital or nursing home facility for sixty consecutive days. After the sixty days, a new benefit period can start. There is no limit to the number of benefit periods a person can have.

The cost of skilled nursing home care varies greatly. The average rate is between $50 and $60 per day or $1,600 and $1,800 per month. Check with your local health care association for recommendations and cost for your area.

Social service agencies can assist with placement and explain the admission process. After a home has been chosen, you may have to put the patient's name on a waiting list. If immediate care is needed, check other community resources for assistance. Some possibilities are home health agencies and day care centers.

## CONVALESCENT HOMES

Convalescent homes may offer the same types of medical and nursing services as skilled nursing homes. However, the care at this type of facility is generally regarded as at the intermediate level. These homes have nursing services, but are less medically oriented and mainly focus on personal care. Patients receive help with bathing, dressing, eating, getting in and out of bed, and walking.

Persons who require less intensive nursing care or who are

---

*Most nursing homes in the United States are not skilled nursing facilities and many skilled nursing facilities are not certified by Medicare.

not capable of caring for their own personal needs may use this type of unit. It is less expensive than a skilled nursing home. The range is between $1,050 and $1,200 per month.

Convalescent homes must be certified by Medicare if Medicare is to pay for the care of any residents. However, when the services the patient receives are mainly personal or custodial, including those described above, Medicare will not pay. Medicare does pay physicians' fees and other medical costs such as physical therapy and outpatient hospital services. Again, make sure the nursing home you select is approved by the federal government standards if you plan to receive benefits.

## RESIDENTIAL HOMES

When persons are able to function independently and yet need or desire some supervision, a residential home provides a clean and safe atmosphere. Individuals in this type of care unit are relieved of the stresses of living alone. Meals and housekeeping services are offered. Generally, patients must be able to get to meals and to toilet without help.

Residents are allowed to live independent lives yet have the security of others around. Supervision and protection are provided, and a variety of social and recreational activities is available. This type of care is the least expensive and allows capable individuals to enjoy life within a less structured atmosphere. Medicare benefits do not support this type of facility. The cost for residential care averages between $500 and $750 per month, again dependent on the location and the area.

## ALTERNATIVES TO NURSING HOME CARE

Some families may want to keep the patient at home as long as possible. Local social service agencies have the names of organizations which help with nursing care; for example, visiting nurses who may help with bathing, or giving medications. Community or fraternal organizations may rent equipment such as hospital beds, wheelchairs, and walkers. Other community organizations may provide transportation. "Meals on wheels" provides one hot meal a day for people who cannot cook for themselves.

Families sometimes do reach a point when someone must stay

at home with a person with dementia. The spouse may choose to retire early to provide the needed care in order to minimize nursing and custodial costs. There are many tradeoffs to consider in this decision. If a spouse elects early retirement to care for a disabled partner, this action affects later financial security because it reduces the years available to work and build up retirement. Also, the able partner must give up the friendship of coworkers and the increased breadth of interest which comes from a job. Eventually the patient will require nursing home care, and the able family member or spouse is left with less potential income in retirement years, and must develop new relationships and interests.

The alternative of hiring nursing care in the home does not work well in our experience unless exceptional help is available. It is extremely difficult to hire dependable caregivers. Also, provision has to be made for days off, vacations and sick days. While agencies will provide nursing help (at the aide level) for about $75 for two shifts, in our experience the quality of the care available is not high. If this course is elected, be alert for any sign of neglect or even abuse of the patient. Expect to try out and discharge several persons before finding two or three who are responsible. Expect to have to take over on short notice because someone does not show up for work.

## WHAT HOMES OFFER AND HOW TO EVALUATE THEM

Sometimes, first impressions may be the best guide. Upon entering the nursing home, what are your first impressions? Is there a disagreeable odor? If a number of patients are sitting together in one large room, is there conversation? Is the staff circulating among the residents or are they talking among themselves over coffee? Do residents have smiles on their faces or are they staring off in space or sleeping? How many nurses are in contact with patients? Are there staff in individual rooms or walking with patients in the halls? Does the nursing staff refer to the patients as Mr. or Mrs. or by their first names? What are your impressions when you visit the dining room and the activity room where the residents watch T.V.?

Check the staffing of the home. What is the staff–patient ratio? Are consultant services and physical and recreational therapists available? Are there regular staff meetings with families? Ask about the staff. Are the nurses registered or practical nurses? Are both types on duty both day and night? How are nurse's aides trained and what is the patient ratio for social workers? Does the nursing home have a current license from the state? Does the administrative staff hold current licenses? Medicare rules are more stringent than most state regulations. Homes are inspected by Medicare and standards must at least meet reasonable minimum standards. Is the home approved for payments from Medicare?

Look at the physical conditions and atmosphere. To prevent accidents and provide safety, are all areas well lighted? Are there handrails in the hallways and grab bars in the bathrooms? Is the furniture sturdy? Does the home meet federal and state fire codes? Are doors to stairways kept closed, and is there an emergency evacuation plan? Do staff and patients practice fire drill exercises on a frequent basis?

Take note of the bedrooms for the residents. Are they pleasant and clean? Do all rooms open onto a hall and is there a window in each room? How many patients are in a room? Is there a closet for each resident? Does each bed have a bell to call the nurse, and is there a drape around the bed for privacy? Are the rooms decorated with bright colors, draperies, attractive furniture? How accessible is the nursing staff to the resident's bedroom? Is there a lounge which can be used for family visits or parties?

Observe the dining room. Is it attractive? Are there windows? Is there a tablecloth on each table and is the table set neatly? Are the residents talking to one another? Are the meals served at the table or cafeteria style and by whom, staff or patients? Does the food look appetizing? Is the kitchen clean and well equipped? Are sanitation rules posted and observed by kitchen workers?

Investigate the other kinds of medical services available. Is the patient's physician allowed to write orders? What kinds of medical records are kept? Are patients' activities charted on a daily basis? Other than medical services, what other kinds of specialists are available? Is there a dentist or optometrist on staff? How does the nursing home provide for medical emergencies? If the need should arise, how close is the nearest hospital, and what transportation is available?

Inquire about the programs available for residents. Is a physical therapist on duty, and is the therapy requested by the physician available to the patient? If a recreational therapist is on staff, are there activities planned outside of the home? How are volunteers used; for example, do they give nursing care or assist in group activities? Is clergy available? Are barbers and beauticians available on site, or are patients transported for these services?

After you have chosen a nursing home to meet the patient's needs and family's standards, the next issue of concern is cost. Families should meet with administrators and social workers to discuss in detail what the financial conditions are. All financial agreements should be in writing, and copies of any agreements given to family members.

Many families need help with the financial burden of nursing care. Seek out insurance agents. Are any benefits available from insurance policies for nursing home care? If the daily rate is not covered, maybe some of the other expenses such as drugs and medical supplies will be covered. Check with local welfare departments and social security offices to explore possibilities for assistance. Also, look into Medicare benefits, if the patient is eligible. Another possibility for care is through private or fraternal organizations. Many fraternal or community organizations own and support nursing home facilities. Do not be afraid to pursue and ask questions.

## INSURANCE AND SOURCES OF FINANCIAL AID

Life insurance policies on the patient should be checked for provisions granting disability waivers of premium particularly if the patient is under age sixty-five. Age sixty-five is the age when disability ends and retirement begins. These waivers cover the cost of premiums when the insured is designated as disabled. This type of coverage is usually provided at very low additional cost on life insurance and mortgage insurance policies at the time of employment. Insurance policies differ, however, and the description of *disability* can vary from "able to do some kind of work" to "unable to ever work again." In the event a diagnosis of dementia is made at an early age, disability insurance premium waivers can save money for the family and keep life insurance policies in force.

Other sources of financial aid include Social Security, Aid to Families with Dependent Children, Disability Income, Medicare, Supplemental Security Insurance, Medicaid, veteran's benefits, and private health insurance.

With the exception of Veterans Administration benefits, other financial resources are intended to provide primarily crisis-oriented or short-term care; consequently, many services are perceived as not being appropriate for Alzheimer's patients who require long-term care. Families must be resourceful and systematically explore any possible financial resource.

## MEDICARE

Medicare is a federal government program for health insurance. The program is for all persons sixty-five and older, some under age sixty-five, and all those who are disabled. Medicare is divided into two categories: medical and hospital insurance. Medicare hospital insurance, sometimes called Part A, can help pay for care received as a patient in a hospital and, after a hospital stay, in a skilled nursing home. Hospital insurance will also help pay for care at home if a home health agency is helping to provide care.

Services covered by Medicare hospital insurance include a semiprivate room, meals, and nursing services. Also included are costs of care in special care units, drugs, laboratory tests, X rays, and medical supplies. Use of appliances such as a wheelchair, operating and recovery room charges, and rehabilitation services come under Medicare, too. Medicare will not pay for television, radio, a telephone in the room, private nurses, or private rooms.

Medicare medical insurance, referred to as Part B, can help pay doctors' bills, including medical–surgical services, diagnostic tests, and procedures that are part of a treatment plan. Outpatient hospital services, such as physical therapy, and medical services and supplies that are not covered under hospital insurance are covered under the medical insurance.

Under Medicare medical insurance, there is a basic payment rule which states that the first $60 in reasonable charges is paid by the patient. This is called the medical insurance deductible and starts again each calendar year. Then medical insurance will cover 80 percent of the charges for any additional services received during the remainder of the year.

Other services and supplies covered by Medicare medical insurance are emergency room services, laboratory and X rays, medical supplies, and drugs. Medical insurance also covers ambulance transportation; however, the ambulance equipment and personnel must meet the requirements of Medicare.

Medical insurance also covers some medical equipment, including oxygen equipment, wheelchairs, and other medically necessary equipment that a doctor prescribes. The equipment may be rented or purchased; however, Medicare will make only monthly payments. The monthly payments will be made until Medicare has paid its share of the purchase price or until the equipment is no longer needed.

Medicare hospital and medical insurance benefits will be paid for home health care of up to 100 visits each calendar year. The patient must require part-time skilled nursing care and be confined to home. A doctor must determine the need for care at home, and periodically review the plan for care. The home health agency involved must be a participant in Medicare. The visits are in addition to the posthospital visits covered by hospital insurance.

Medicare payments are handled by private insurance companies under contract with the government. Under the law, there are some limits for submitting medical insurance claims. Claims for service must be submitted within fifteen months of the time of service. However, the provisions of Medicare and Medicaid are constantly being reviewed and changed. For information in your area, contact the Medicare carrier or any social security office.

# CHAPTER 8
# PRACTICAL MATTERS

Much of the material contained in this chapter is practical knowledge which we think will be useful: what to tell children, relatives and neighbors; what legal rights and responsibilities are involved; insurance, retirement plans and social security; working up a family history. We often will be unable to be specific because every situation is unique. States offer different types of services and have their own laws, so legal issues are especially complex. Inquiries of state level social service departments may have to be made, and for most families, an attorney will be needed.

## CHILDREN IN THE HOME

Children living in a household where a person is showing signs of dementia will be well aware of the changes, and know that a problem exists. At the onset some children do not understand or know how to react to the situation. Sometimes they understand only the effect it has upon them and other family members.

The able parent's best course is to be truthful with children, at least those at an age of understanding, and to tell them exactly what is happening. The problem which is, or soon will be, affecting the entire family cannot be hidden or covered up. Also, the parent should tell the children what the doctors have said might be expected to happen and, if possible, should make an appointment for the children to see one of the doctors to ask questions. In the long run, they will be better able to accept the person with dementia and the effects of the disease if they know the basic facts.

Indeed, children sometimes cope with a nonfunctioning parent or grandparent better than do adults. Children may not make the demands that adults do. They don't converse on abstract topics. But like all of us, children can become angry and frustrated at the failures of the ill person, and they may find it difficult to understand the lack of interest such persons often have in their child's or grandchild's world. Yet, in general, children do very well with mentally incompetent adults. They may indeed become a parent by telling the patient what to do and when to do it, and by reacting to situations where judgment is required. Children quickly learn the *do's* and *don't's* of handling their demented parent or grandparent. If the affected individual is in a possibly dangerous situation, children may step in and protect them from potential harm.

A special problem for children may be embarrassment in front of their friends. They may not want friends to visit the home because they are afraid that the person with dementia will do or say something strange. Concerned about what other kids will say, some children choose not to tell their friends. Others do. Parents should not push the child on this matter, but might encourage the child to talk freely about the problems they are encountering. Then allow them time to learn to cope with the situation in their own way.

Placing a parent or grandparent in a nursing home, or even making the decision for nursing home placement, is hard for the entire family. When the time does come, and placement has been made, the caregiving family feels a sense of relief. This reaction is normal and children may particularly be affected by the loss; however, the normal pattern of everyday living usually quickly returns.

Parents find it very difficult to accept children telling them that they do not want to visit the nursing home. This is a very normal reaction, and children should not be made to feel guilty or pushed into making visits. Give the children time, and when they are comfortable they will make the right decision. When the children choose to go with the family for a visit, the visit should be kept short because the parent's or grandparent's progressive deterioration can be very upsetting. Many times these children do develop a sense of understanding and compassion after the experience. After the condition has worsened to the point that the ill person does not recognize visitors, we advise against visits by younger children.

## WHAT TO TELL RELATIVES AND NEIGHBORS

Be truthful even if it is difficult. Often when a spouse or child must explain the diagnosis to relatives, they are faced with one of two reactions. Either the family is very supportive of the spouse or the family member who is caring for the patient, and understands the situation, or the family refuses to accept the fact that something is wrong with their relative. They may blame the situation on other circumstances: "You have made the person unhappy"; or "if you had fed the person properly"; or "if you had been more attentive, this would never have happened."

Families who are fortunate to have the support of the other members may still feel that they have not done all that is possible. Therefore, support of the entire family is vital. That is why all of the information about the patient should be shared. Doctors' visits, consultations with specialists, hospital evaluations, and the daily happenings should be circulated among all family members.

If the spouse or child does not carry the entire load and allows input from other members, this may relieve some of the guilt that may be associated with the decisions made concerning the consequences of the illness. Ultimately, however, the major decisions do fall upon the caregiver.

To give other family members some idea of the caregiver's demanding job, ask them to care for the patient for a few days while the caregiver gets some needed rest. They will become more aware of the demands of caring for a demented person and perhaps will better understand why the primary caregiver has made certain decisions. Share the literature that is available with all family members and invite them to attend an Alzheimer's support group meeting where they can ask questions and visit with others who are experiencing the same kind of problems.

As much as families try to keep the patient indoors and not

tell the neighbors, neighbors are probably well aware of the problems. The patient may have been roaming the neighborhood asking for help or money to get away, or just being a nuisance. The neighbors may also have become involved when they found the patient wandering. Families are surprised and embarrassed by this public behavior.

Again, be truthful. Tell the neighbors exactly what has happened. Also, tell them about the illness so they will not be afraid of the patient and will be better prepared to handle a situation if the need should arise.

Most often families will find that neighbors are thoughtful and very helpful. They will call when they see the patient wandering about or doing something dangerous. They can provide moral support to the caregiver by visiting. If the patient should become difficult to control, neighbors are close and can be available at a moment's notice.

## COMPETENCE AND LEGAL RESPONSIBILITY

Financial problems are often an indicator of the early stages of dementia. More than the usual number of checks may be recorded incorrectly or may have been written and not recorded at all. Problems with simple addition and subtraction are not uncommon.

In addition to poor records, families may find that unwise financial decisions have been made. Sometimes these decisions have long-term effects on the financial situation; for example, the affected person may have sold property or given away jewelry, furs, or other expensive personal items. Therefore, families should gather all financial documents together and do this in the early stages of the illness. They should review savings and investment accounts and thoroughly understand assets or financial commitments. This is important because within a short period of time the person affected may well be unable to provide an understandable history of financial transactions, let alone manage them.

Removing legal and financial responsibilities from a person undergoing the early stages of dementia may be met by hostility. The patient may become overly suspicious and mistrustful, telling friends and neighbors that the family is stealing, even calling the police to ask for help. If resistance develops, it may be passive; family members may be able to assume enough authority to exercise *de facto* control. In many cases, however, there may be no choice except obtaining legal control; bills must be paid and family assets need to be protected. In general, hostility based on loss of financial authority is short-lived. Patients are relieved from anxiety produced by mental tasks that they cannot manage and may even be grateful.

No matter what the course, at some point the demented person will be no longer capable of making financial decisions. If this person has been the main wage earner and has handled the family's financial operations, the spouse or other designated person of the family will have to assume the responsibility. Legal assistance will be required.

In order for a spouse or any family member to act on behalf of an ill person, legal action through the court process is required. This is true even if the ill individual is unable to understand what is happening or has become physically unable to sign documents. The usual process to obtain this authority is through a *conservatorship, power of attorney,* or *guardianship.*

**Conservatorship** A conservatorship is initiated by an individual to protect, guide and maintain his financial affairs. If the disease is in its early stages, the individual affected may appoint another person or financial agency to act in his behalf through a conservatorship. Sometimes people realize that they are losing their ability to manage financial arrangements and initiate this process. A conservatorship is granted by a court and is continually under the supervision of the courts.

**Power of Attorney** A power of attorney is a written statement legally authorizing one person to act on behalf of another. In addition to financial management, the authority can include buying and selling of real estate and managing of property. However, the person who gives the power of attorney must know what is being done and understand its significance.

**Guardianship** A guardianship is a legal process which results in appointment of an individual or agency to handle the affairs of an individual who can no longer function independently. A guardian can be a family member or institution appointed by the court. The guardian must protect and take care of the person and property of one who is found incapable of managing his own affairs. Usually a family member can institute this process, but the court will maintain supervisory rights over the guardian and institution appointed.

For the spouse, another aspect to consider is joint ownership of property. In most cases joint ownership is a great advantage because the property is in both names; therefore, in most instances the able partner will take over the ownership and manage the assets.

Even the simple process of filling out joint income tax returns may become complicated if one partner cannot sign the form. In such cases, obtain a "Power of Attorney" tax form, which gives specific authority to act for another person in all matters pertaining to taxes. The form is available from any branch office of the Internal Revenue Service and state tax office. While the patient remains competent to consent and to continue to file joint tax forms, complete and fill out as many power of attorney forms as may be needed for years in advance.

When nursing home care is required, assets still in the patient's name will have to be used to pay for care in that home. Sometimes young dependents are involved; their care should be considered. An attorney may be able to help conserve assets for their needs.

Title 19 of the Social Security Act grants monies to states for medical assistance programs. The law also deals with the liability of spouses and other family members for the cost of long-term care such as is often required by persons with dementia. This law has been interpreted differently by states, but basically it defines the financial responsibilities of families and the limits to that responsibility. For example, persons must qualify for low income and disability status under social security or state criteria.

Federal agencies do not have contact with recipients or providers of these medical assistance services although they do determine eligibility through social security offices. The programs themselves are operated by state agencies. Thus, financial help for long-term care can best be accomplished through social service departments at the state level.

The best advice to any family is to consult an attorney and, if possible, try to find one who has some knowledge of the disease.

## INSURANCE AND INSURABILITY

Insurance coverage for persons who become disabled such as those with dementia is a major concern. Most of us do not think about insurance benefits or coverage until we need them. When families are faced with little or no coverage, they panic. They may, on impulse, buy any policy that they can get and be sorry when they try to use it.

Most persons, while employed, are insured by a company health care plan. If they should become disabled and cannot work, that insurance coverage will usually provide protection for one additional year. After that time they may have the option to convert the policy and pay the premiums themselves. But in most cases to convert from a group policy to single coverage is costly and may not be within the person's financial means.

If they cannot pay for insurance coverage, persons are eligible to apply for county assistance. If they are fortunate enough to live in a state which provides a comprehensive health plan, they may be covered under this type of insurance. There is, however, usually a six month waiting period before a comprehensive health policy provides benefits.

Most insurance policies contain a clause which states that any predisposing illness, such as progressive dementia, is not covered. Such policies are of no value to the person with dementia. After the diagnosis is made and recorded in Medicare records, for practical purposes, the ill person is no longer insurable. State health plans, however, cannot have an exemption clause based on predisposing illness, so this may be a source of financial help. Unfortunately, state health plans do not exist in all states. Families should check with their local insurance board to find out what options for health care coverage are available in the state in which they reside.

Health Maintenance Organizations (HMOs) may be a source of help for persons receiving Medicare benefits. The Health Care Financing Administration, which administers HMOs, also administers the Medicare program and encourages Medicare beneficiaries to consider joining an HMO which has a Medicare contract because services offered by such an HMO will be covered by Medicare. Many HMOs offer additional services for an additional premium.

Like an insurance company, an HMO pays the costs for health

care (which includes both the doctor and hospital) for a monthly premium. There are two types of HMOs: those operating from one central location and those operating from the offices of individual doctors. The advantages of joining an HMO include availability of all services needed, such as doctor's services, hospital care, laboratory, X rays, and emergency care. Persons using the services of an HMO must continue to pay the monthly Medicare medical insurance (Medicare Part B). For most people, this premium is deducted from the monthly social security check. Medicare interprets the premium paid to an HMO as paid to coinsurer, and therefore provides for payment of charges for deductibles.

As families investigate various types of medical insurance and coverage, they should be wary of policies that offer nursing home coverage. These types of policies are available and have been in existence for some time. However, most of the policies will have a clause which states that the policy can only be used for skilled nursing care in a nursing home. In order to process the claim, the patient's doctor must state that skilled nursing care is required. These types of policies are closely monitored and if the insurance company determines that the patient is not receiving twenty-four-hour, seven-day-a-week care administered by a registered nurse they will refuse to pay benefits. This type of policy may also carry the clause that the policy cannot be used for six months, and after this six month waiting period, the policy will pay the costs only for 120 days.

Medicare benefits, which include medical costs, are available for persons who are disabled, under age sixty-five, and who have been receiving disability checks from social security for two years. These benefits provide hospital insurance protection at no charge to the individual; however, persons who want medical insurance pay a monthly premium.

## RETIREMENT PLANS

Retirement plans may be provided by employers to supplement income in retirement years. If employees have worked the minimum number of years required by the plan, they are entitled to benefits, even if the illness forced early retirement. Such benefits often begin immediately. Even if not eligible for full retirement benefits, a person who is disabled may be eligible for some benefits under most retirement plans. These benefits may include hospitalization and life insurance. After applying for the benefits, they are also eligible to apply for disability payments under the provisions of social security. (Guidelines for disability benefits will be discussed in the next section.) Because of the long-term effects of dementing illness, affected persons will be better off financially if they apply for benefits as early as possible.

Persons choosing to retire at an early age usually receive benefits at a reduced rate. Although people are eligible for retirement at age sixty-two, full benefits are based on retirement at age sixty-five. If application for social security benefits is made before age sixty-five, the reduction of monthly payment depends on the number of monthly checks received before age sixty-five. However, the same total benefits will be received provided the average lifespan is lived. Payments are also reduced for a widow, widower, husband, or wife of a full retiree who starts receiving social security payments before age sixty-five.

## SOCIAL SECURITY BENEFITS

Social security provides a continuing income when family earnings are reduced or stopped because of retirement, disability, or death. This program will nearly always be available to persons with dementing illness. To be eligible to receive cash benefits, a minimum amount of work under social security must have been done. The exact amount of work credit depends on age and quarter when coverage began.

Social security credit is measured in quarters of coverage. There are four quarters of coverage for each year. Persons who stop working under social security before they have earned enough credit are not eligible to receive benefits. The credit will remain on their record, however, and if they return to work under social security, they may add credits to those already earned.

Work credit for disability benefits is different if a person becomes disabled at age thirty-one or later. For persons thirty-one or older, eligibility requires only five years of work credit out of the ten years prior to the onset of disability. For persons younger than thirty-one, additional credit may be needed depending on age and date of onset of disability.

Under social security guidelines, a person is considered disabled when a physical or mental condition exists which prevents substantial work, and when the condition is expected to last, or has lasted, for twelve months, or is likely to result in death. Applicants must provide medical evidence of severity of the condition and prove that the condition prevents working.

Persons receiving disability benefits can also receive money for children who are unmarried and under eighteen years old, or who are unmarried and attending school full time. A spouse is also eligible if sixty-two or older.

Disability benefits begin after five full months. Since no benefits will be paid for those first five months, disability must exist for a full six months before the first payment can be received. Apply for benefits as soon as possible after disability can be established. Back payments are limited to the twelve months preceding the month during which application was made.

Another federal program, Supplemental Security Income (SSI), is provided for persons who are disabled or who have little or no income and resources. This program supplements income even when income is available from other sources, including social security.

Although the Social Security Administration administers SSI, SSI is not the same as social security. SSI payments come from the general funds of the U.S. Treasury, while social security benefits are contributed by workers, employers, and self-employed persons.

Under SSI, state, federal, and local governments work together. However, the federal government administers this program through the Social Security Administration. In addition, states supplement federal payments by providing Medicaid, food stamps, and social rehabilitation support.

The financial assistance offered by SSI is relatively free of restrictions. Unlike welfare, those who receive this assistance can retain their own home; there is no lien requirement. Personal property, including an automobile, may also be kept; values are reasonable. This federal program does not require support from relatives.

For patients in institutions, there are three exceptions to the rule concerning eligibility for SSI payments:

1. SSI payments may be denied if the recipient resides in a public or private health care facility which is receiving payments from Medicaid for giving care.

2. The payment may be reduced if the recipient is living in a publicly operated community residence which serves no more than sixteen people.
3. The patient may not be eligible if he is staying in a public institution primarily to attend approved education or vocational training.

Those receiving SSI must apply for any other money benefits which may be due under social security. If other benefits are received, SSI payments can be reduced. However, the state may augment SSI payments without penalty if the state's payment is made on a regular basis and is based on need.

For additional information about social security benefits, Medicare, or SSI, contact any social security office. Look in the phone directory under Social Security Administration or ask for information at a post office.

## HOW TO WORK UP YOUR FAMILY HISTORY

Families who suspect other cases of dementing illness among their relatives may become concerned about possible genetic risks. They may then consider seeking genetic counseling.

The counselor will want to know about the medical history of the entire family. This is done by gathering information from as many family members as possible. Compiling the family medical history is not much different from constructing a family tree. However, the genetic counselor is much more interested in clinical information and causes of death than in the name of a great-great-grandfather.

The people seeking the counseling will do most of the work in gathering information. First they must consult with other family members to complete the genealogical chart. Of course, a main question is if anyone in the family has or had the symptoms of dementia. This may be difficult to determine. At least find out whether or not relatives had been able to care for themselves until their final illness.

This basic information will be needed about parents, grandparents, aunts, uncles, brothers, and sisters of the person affected. How many of these relatives are living and what is their health status? If they are deceased, where did they die and when? If you know in which state death occurred, you can write to that state board of health and get a copy of the death certificate. (Appendix D has a complete list of where to write and the cost of obtaining the certificate.) When sending for a certificate, include the name of the deceased, his parents' names and the place and date of death. It usually takes about five or six weeks to get a copy of the certificate. If information is incomplete, the search may take longer and there may be an additional charge.

A main reason for wanting to get copies of death certificates is to find out if an autopsy had been performed. Sometimes, however, the entry for autopsy is left blank. This usually means that one was not performed. If there is a doubt, check to see where death took place. If it took place outside a hospital, an autopsy most likely was not performed. However, if it took place in a hospital, records can be checked. Sometimes after a period of time (usually seven years), hospitals will destroy patient records. But if the hospital has a pathology laboratory, some record of the autopsy will still exist. Maybe even some of the autopsy tissue will still be available and may be sent to a neuropathologist for diagnostic study. A relative can obtain medical records with the procedures described under autopsies in Chapter 4.

The cause of death listed on death certificates is generally not reliable. However, some diagnoses do suggest progressive dementia, for example, presenile dementia, organic brain syndrome, or senility. The duration of the condition will usually be estimated on the certificate and, by considering all of the available evidence, reasonable diagnostic conclusion may be possible. A genetic counselor or knowledgeable physician may be needed to interpret the evidence available to you.

# CHAPTER 9
# THE FUTURE

We have described diseases which have beset our species throughout its history. For those witnessing their effects on someone they love, this book promises little immediate relief. We think that some of the practical tips we offered may be helpful; but they only peck at the surface of monstrous tragedies. The hope is for the future, and it lies in biomedical research. Look in that direction and the horizon glows brightly indeed.

For perspective, briefly review the progress of the brain sciences over the past two decades. Twenty years ago, virtually nothing was known about the brain. Neurotransmission had been studied at the junction between nerve and muscle. The tracks of the spinal cord had been described and the path taken by messages to and from the lower brain to peripheral structures, such as muscles, had been fairly well worked out. But the brain itself was an unknown black box, or rather a box containing white and gray structures: gray, the bodies of nerve cells; white, the tracks running between gray structures. Every gray or white feature which could be discriminated had been given a name—medical students memorized each of them but knew little more than what to call them. By studying brains damaged by strokes or other injuries, the function of some structures of the brain had been inferred, but our ignorance was abysmal.

We can hardly say that neuroscience research has been marked by a series of brilliant breakthroughs since that time; progress has rather been slow and slogging, but it has been steady. Today, as never before, biology and, perhaps, especially the neurosciences seem poised for a series of those advances as dramatic as any in the history of science. To illustrate the possibilities, we will describe an overview of recent developments in genetics, a fundamental biological science closely related to neuroscience, and two technological advances which promise revolutionary changes in our capacity to study the living brain. Over the next twenty years we can confidently expect a much clearer understanding of the biology of the brain and, we fully believe, effective treatment of progressive dementias.

## GENETICS

The continuing revolution in genetic research is at the molecular level. Its subject matter is DNA, RNA and proteins. It is well known that DNA contains the genetic code, that a gene is a long strand of DNA, and that the message of the gene is transferred from DNA to RNA. RNA then serves as a template upon which proteins are assembled. DNA, through RNA, dictates the structure and thereby the function of proteins. In turn, proteins do the work of life. Many proteins made by this process have structures designed eventually to incorporate minerals, fats, sugars or other small molecules, but proteins are the organizing framework. They are our structural pieces and they conduct and control ongoing life processes.

A maladaptive change in DNA constitutes a genetic fault. It may be expressed through altered structure of a protein which makes it ineffective at its assigned task. Or the fault may be expressed in one of the myriad ways that proteins are changed after they are made. These changes are effected by other proteins; therefore, the whole of the process of change is controlled ultimately by DNA. Proteins may be cut into smaller segments; large molecules may be assembled out of several smaller ones. A fault may occur in the way proteins are put into their working positions, or are deactivated when damaged or no longer needed; or the protein simply may be present in the wrong amount given the environment in which the organism is functioning.

What the last few years have brought is no less than the development of techniques that seem certain to produce a comprehensive map of the DNA of all organisms, including humans. This includes the detailed molecular structure of all variants of DNA (there are several variants of many proteins and so there are corresponding variants at the DNA level), and the relative position of all genes along the chains of DNA.

The implications are enormous. Science will soon know the structure and location of genes associated with human diseases including, of course, the progressive dementias. The path of discovery has been explored far enough to be sure that it will lead to that end.

First, the structure and location of a large number of *markers* must be discovered. The markers, themselves genes or the products of genes, serve as fixed points upon which to base the map. Genes can be located between two markers and most likely closer to one than to the other. The process is sequential; each located gene becomes a new marker and that makes it easier to locate other genes. Progress in this quest, which is well under way, can be expected to accelerate. It will not be done cheaply or easily, and no doubt many surprises await, but there is no longer reason to doubt that biological science will accomplish this immense feat.

Picking out genes associated with progressive dementias might proceed along several possible lines. But the basic method will be systematic comparison of the genes from victims with the map of genetic structure which will have been built up. (Genes from a living person can be studied quite conveniently in a sample of blood.)

## POSITRON-EMITTING TOMOGRAPHY

Even after a gene, or genes, associated with a disease has been located, its DNA code discovered, and the product of the gene, a protein, is isolated in a test tube, a huge task remains before the information gained can be effectively used. We would still not know the place occupied by the protein in the ongoing life processes of the body. What does the protein do? How does it get to where it must do whatever it does? With what other molecules does it work? Answers to such questions will be needed to provide medicine with the depth of understanding needed to engineer effective interventions into the process.

Until very recently, the belief that we would ever gain that knowledge about the living functioning human brain required unbridled optimism, or unquestioning faith, or both. It now seems that optimism and faith were warranted. New techniques have been developed which make it possible to watch the living brain in action. The most dramatic of these techniques is positron-emitting tomography (PET), as it is now widely known.

The positron is a positively charged electron with a very short life in nature. As soon as it encounters an electron, which is negatively charged, both types of electrons are destroyed and two photons are produced. The two photons have a peculiar property. When produced, they speed away from one another at the speed of light in almost exactly opposite directions. Their combined path therefore is a straight line. Now, if a positron is attached to some molecule used by brain tissue, such as oxygen or glucose, the brain will emit photons from the areas which are using oxygen or glucose, and the greater the concentration of oxygen or glucose, the greater the number of photons released.

PET technology depends on the physical properties just described. The positron–electron collision produces two photons which depart from each other in opposite directions; their path is a continuous straight line with little deviation. If the patient's head is surrounded by materials which can detect photons, and if the detecting materials are arranged so that only simultaneous *hits* by two photons are recorded, then it becomes possible, with essential help from computers, to calculate a line, referenced to the anatomy of the brain and skull, along which a given positron was destroyed.

In current application, the patient's head is surrounded by individual detectors arranged in three to five layers or *arrays.* Each layer can produce a separate image of photon emission, so the brain can be seen at different levels, much as permitted by the CAT scan. Each layer contains over 300 individual detectors. The images produced show the relative amounts of positron-containing substance at specific locations in brain tissue.

In the case of glucose or oxygen, the PET scan image reflects the brain's overall metabolic activity. A few preliminary results of studies of progressive dementias have already been reported. In DAT the activity of the outer parts of the brain is greatly reduced while in Huntington's disease, the outer parts of the brain are normally active but certain internal structures show diminished activity. Of course, such findings are important clues, and they suggest that PET may one day help with the problem of diagnosis which we have described.

The great promise of PET seems to be in labeling with positrons substances involved in more specific reactions rather than gross overall energy metabolism. This should eventually allow fine distinctions to be made concerning the brain's most subtle reactions. In order to do this, other substances important to brain function will have to be labeled with positrons. Choline is a possibility; so are other raw materials used by the brain, such as the amino acid tryptophan. Hormones are likely targets. So are drugs. By using such labeled materials as probes, the functioning brain may slowly become accessible to analysis.

## NUCLEAR MAGNETIC RESONANCE

PET is not the only new technology emerging from the laboratories promising to help dissect brain function. Another is nuclear magnetic resonance (NMR), which depends on strong magnetic fields to yield detailed three-dimensional replicas of solid objects, including the brain. The image produced depends on the chemical and physical properties of the material being scanned. The process is very sensitive to small changes in these properties so that gray matter can actually be distinguished from white matter in images from the living brain.

At present, NMR is being explored mainly through studies of anatomical changes in living brain. It produces extremely clear detailed images which already are proving useful in diagnosis. However, the promise of the technique extends far beyond anatomy. NMR images can be based on several different kinds of physical and chemical information. Therefore several different images of the same subject can be produced, with each image containing different information. By choosing suitable chemicals to produce images, it will be possible to learn to understand fundamental metabolic process in living subjects.

The wonder of PET and NMR to those who have followed the neurosciences is the promise they offer of getting past the skull into the workings of the living brain. Moreover, both techniques seem to be entirely safe to human subjects. There is no reason to expect that NMR would pose biological risks. PET does entail administration of radioactive material. But the dose is very small and will be made smaller still as techniques and equipment improve. Also, positron-emitting compounds have very short half-lives—typically one to two minutes—so the radiation does not persist.

The major drawback is expense. A PET installation can easily run from two to five million dollars and NMR not much less. In addition, teams of highly qualified professionals are required to operate these extremely complex and sophisticated systems. Biomedical research does cost money—a lot of money. But those who pay taxes to support research, or who contribute to organizations such as those described in this book, might find it comforting to reflect that the amount spent on research is a minute proportion of the amount now being spent on treatments, which are largely ineffective, or for custodial care. Support of research is a wise investment in the best humanistic sense. For millions of us, it is our single best hope.

# APPENDIX A

# MEDICAL LABORATORY TESTS USED IN INVESTIGATIONS OF POSSIBLE DEMENTIAS

These are tests likely to be ordered by physicians when doing a diagnostic work-up of a case of dementia. The list of tests is intended to be only a general guide. The diagnostic trail may branch off because of the results of a physical examination or other investigations, and additional tests to assess specific systems may be ordered. Some of the listed tests may not be needed in particular cases because other evidence eliminates problems in specific areas.

The following list includes; tests often ordered as screens on admission to a hospital or as part of a comprehensive outpatient examination, as well as a brief explanation of the purpose for each:

| Test | Purpose |
| --- | --- |
| Complete blood count (CBC) | Will detect anemia or cancers of the blood system. Will focus suspicion on pernicious anemia or chronic |

| | |
|---|---|
| | infections and lead to further investigations. |
| Urinalysis | May detect diabetes or diseases of the kidney or liver. Infections of the urinary system may be especially troublesome in elderly persons. |
| Electrolytes | Tested in blood serum. These are salts which are present normally in precisely regulated amounts. Abnormalities in their concentration may cause mental symptoms, though not dementia. Their main importance, however, is as an indicator of major disease of other systems, especially endocrine and kidney. |
| Endocrine screen | Mainly for abnormality of thyroid. |
| Serologic tests for syphilis | Done on blood or CSF or both. |
| Blood urea nitrogen (BUN) | Screen for kidney disease. |
| Bilirubin | Elevated in liver disease. |
| Glucose | Elevated in blood in diabetes. |

Tests in addition to usual screens when dementia is being investigated are the following:

| | |
|---|---|
| Erythrocyte sedimentation rate (ESR or sed rate) | Is generally positive in chronic infections which may otherwise present |

| | |
|---|---|
| | little evidence of their presence in elderly persons. Will be positive in inflammations of arteries which may compromise blood supply to the brain. |
| Vitamins (in blood) | Folic acid, vitamin $B_{12}$, nicotinic acid will be deficient in chronic malnutrition due to neglect, alcoholism, or specific metabolic diseases. |
| Blood and urine screens for drugs | Will detect and identify minute concentrations of virtually all drugs likely to cause trouble, in some cases days after their administration. |
| Cerebral spinal fluid | Syphilis in the brain may not be detected in the blood. Amount of protein, sugar and number of cells present (normally no cells are present in CSF) may lead doctors to suspect tumor, infections, or blood vessel disease in the brain which in turn may lead to further investigative tests. |
| Endocrine tests (free thyroxine, thyroxine uptake) | If screening tests or physical findings contain the smallest hint of endocrine abnormality, other tests will likely be done. |

## PSYCHOLOGICAL TESTS

The Wechsler Adult Intelligence Scale, generally called simply the WAIS, is frequently administered when dementia is a diagnostic consideration. The WAIS consists of eleven subtests, each separately scored. Some sample questions from various subtests follow:

1. Why are dark clothes warmer than light-colored clothes?
2. What should you do if while in the movies you were the first person to see smoke and fire?
3. A man with $18 spends $7.50. How much does he have left?
4. In what way are an egg and a seed alike?

The most direct test of recent memory in the WAIS is the *digit span* subtest which is made up of two parts, *digits forward* and *digits backward.* The examiner starts with three digits, for example, 5, 8, 2, presented orally which the subject must repeat back immediately. The number of digits is increased by one after each successful trial to a maximum of nine. Digits backward requires the subject to reverse the order presented by the examiner, for example, 7, 5, 8, 3, 6 requires a response of 6, 3, 8, 5, 7.

In other subtests, blocks must be correctly placed to form a specified design or pictures of human forms correctly assembled.

Typically in progressive dementia, the sections depending on memory such as digit span, and those requiring a more abstract attitude such as block design, are relatively more severely affected than tests based mainly on previously learned vocabulary.

Another test frequently used is the Wechsler Memory Scale which uses the digit span subtest of the WAIS plus additional tests of memory: remembering details from a story recited by the examiner or pairs of words, some related, for example, rose–flower, and some unrelated, for example, obey–inch. In the paired word test, the examiner first presents a list of ten pairs of words and then only the first word of each pair. The subject is then asked to supply the second word of the pair.

In our clinical work we use the following short test which we have found to be adequate for repeated assessment of patients over several years. It is made up of parts of several tests plus some features added as a result of our experience. However, it is useful as a rough guide only and in no sense can it be used to replace the complete psychometric battery professionally administered.

1. Examiner: "I am going to tell you a short story. Remember all that you can about it. Just after I finish, I will ask you to repeat the story back to me. Then about fifteen minutes after that, I will ask you to repeat the story again. Here is the story:

   An airliner with 106 people on board was on its way to Tulsa from Cleveland. A careless passenger started a small fire with a cigarette in a lavatory. But a very efficient stewardess put the fire out and the plane landed safely."

*Scoring:* One point for each of the following details mentioned.

1. airliner
2. 106 people aboard
3. from Cleveland
4. to Tulsa
5. fire—cigarette
6. lavatory
7. efficient stewardess
8. safe landing

Immediate recall: Normal is five to eight details, but more important is the loss of information over fifteen minutes. Normally no more than one detail is lost—that is, a subject scoring seven on immediate recall will normally get six, seven or even eight after fifteen minutes. Over several months, the retention of a person suffering a progressive dementia will decline until only irregularly will a detail or two be recalled after fifteen minutes.

2. Examiner: "Subtract 7 from 100." If the answer is "93," the subject is asked to continue subtracting 7's from each previous answer. Give one point for each correct subtraction until 30 is reached or until 10 answers have been given. Although this may seem a simple task, any impairment of intellectual functioning may be readily apparent as subjects attempt it.
3. Examiner shows subject wristwatch and asks:
   1. "What is this?"
   2. Pointing to band—"What is this?"
   3. Pointing to stem—"What is this?"
   4. Pointing to dial—"What is this?"
   5. Pointing to hand—"What is this?"

*Scoring:* Two points for each correct answer.

4. Subject is asked to draw the face of a clock set to 11:10. Even in early dementia, those affected have great difficulty placing the minute hand on 2; rather, they often try to place it on 10. Ten points if both hands are correctly placed.
5. Subject is shown a card with five unrelated words on it (card, broom, mutton, snarl, haul) and asked to remember the words. Subject is also shown a card with five fruits named on it, (pear, apple, orange, plum, apricot). Dementing persons usually do much worse than normals on the list of fruits presumably because they do not use the relatedness of the objects named as memory aids.

*Scoring:* One point for each unrelated word and two points for each related word both for immediate recall and after fifteen minutes.

It is possible to score seventy-six points. There is no normal score. The test is useful only to follow the progress of an illness. By the time scores are in the range 15–25, most persons are so impaired intellectually that they will require full-time supervision. But we have seen gravely impaired persons score up to 35 points.

# APPENDIX B

# ALZHEIMER'S DISEASE AND RELATED DISORDERS ASSOCIATION, IN U.S.A.

U.S.A.
NATIONAL HEADQUARTERS
360 North Michigan Ave.
Chicago, Illinois 60626
(312) 853-3060

Chapters as of April, 1983

**ARIZONA**

PHOENIX: 5821 E. Bloomfield Rd.
Scottsdale, AZ 85254 (602) 948-6418

TUCSON: P.O. Box 17616
Tucson, AZ 85731 (602) 623-8208

**CALIFORNIA**

LOS ANGELES: 11321 Iowa Ave.
Suite 9
Los Angeles, CA 90025 (213) 473-1446

ORANGE COUNTY: 210 Via Cordova
Newport Beach, CA 92663
(714) 631-0245

PENINSULA: 457 Kingsley Ave.
Palo Alto, CA 94301 (415) 494-6110 or
(415) 325-0222

SACRAMENTO: 6253 Watt Ave.
North Highland, CA 95660 (916) 988-9319

SAN DIEGO: 1305 Diamond St.
San Diego, CA 92109 (619) 272-6030

SANTA BARBARA: (Tri-County Area),
3735-A San Remo Dr.
Santa Barbara, CA 93105 (805) 682-5207

**COLORADO**

DENVER: Rose Medical Center
4567 E. 9 Ave.
Denver, CO 80220 (303) 393-7675

**DISTRICT OF COLUMBIA**

METRO WASHINGTON: 819 Aster Blvd.
Rockville, MD 20850
(301) 424-9420

**FLORIDA**

BROWARD COUNTY 9301 Sunrise Lake Blvd.
#109
Sunrise Lake, FL 33322
(305) 741-3984

DAYTONA BEACH: 1282 Mayflower Dr.
Daytona Beach, FL 32019
(904) 767-3757

FORT MYERS (Lee County): Lee Mental Health Center, Inc.
2789 Ortiz Ave. S.E.
P.O. Box 06137
Ft. Myers, FL 33906
(813) 334-3537

JACKSONVILLE: 848 Glynlea Rd.
Jacksonville, FL 32216 (904) 724-1447

MANATEE and
SARASOTA COUNTIES: 585 Yawl Lane
Longboat Key, FL 33507 (813)
383-7870

6303 Sun Eagle Lane
Bradenton, FL 33507
(813) 755-4331

**GEORGIA**

ATLANTA: Wesley Woods Campus
1817 Clifton Rd., NE
Atlanta, GA 30029 (404) 633-8759

4764 La Vista Rd.
Tucker, GA 30084 (404) 491-8969

**HAWAII**

HONOLULU: Ward Warehouse, Bldg. D,
Upper Level
1050 Alta Moana Blvd.
Honolulu, HI 96816 (808) 732-1924

**ILLINOIS**

CHICAGO, ETHS: Rm. S-217
1600 Dodge St.
Evanston, IL 60204 (312) 864-0045

**INDIANA**

SOUTH BEND: 2113 Beverly Place
South Bend, IN 46616 (219) 233-4444

**IOWA**

DES MOINES: Iowa Methodist Medical Center
1200 Pleasant St.
Des Moines, IA 50308 (515) 283-6431

**KANSAS**

KANSAS CITY: 10108 W. 96 St. #B
Overland Park, KS 66212 (913) 492-5228

**KENTUCKY**

LOUISVILLE: 6607 Watch Hill Rd.
Louisville, KY 40228 (502) 239-9329

**MARYLAND**

BALTIMORE: P.O. Box 9751
Baltimore, MD 21204 (301) 792-7800
Ext. 7224

**MASSACHUSETTS**

MASSACHUSETTS: Boston University School of Medicine
80 E. Concord St.
Boston, MA 02118 (617) 247-5941

**MICHIGAN**

ANN ARBOR: 1225 Astor Dr., #222
Ann Arbor, MI 48104 (313) 662-6638

DETROIT: 725 S.Adams, Ste. L-6 (313) 540-2373 or
Birmingham, MI 48011 (313) 332-4110

FLINT and
GENESSEE COUNTY: 514 E. Main St.
Flushing, MI 48433 (313) 659-4435

GRAND RAPIDS: P.O. Box 1646 (616) 456-5664 or
Grand Rapids, MI 49505 (616) 245-5735
(616) 243-0231

MID-MICHIGAN: 9370 Rosebush Rd.
Mt. Pleasant, MI 48858 (517) 465-6602

**MINNESOTA**

BLOOMINGTON: 8900 Queen Ave. South
Bloomington, MN 55431 (612) 888-7653

## MISSOURI

ST. LOUIS: Washington University
School of Medicine
Box 8111
660 S. Euclid Ave.
St. Louis, MO 63110 (314) 454-2384

## NEBRASKA

LINCOLN: 4600 Valley Rd.
Lincoln, NE 68510 (402) 489-6513

OMAHA: P.O. Box 14933
Omaha, NE 68124 (402) 334-0506 or (402) 399-9069

## NEVADA

LAS VEGAS: Charleston Convalescent Center
2035 Charleston Blvd.
Las Vegas, NV 89102 (702) 386-7980

## NEW MEXICO

ALBUQUERQUE: 1027 Pampas Dr. S.E.
Albuquerque, NM 87108 (505) 299-8223 or (505) 266-6621

## NEW YORK

ALBANY: 87 Brookline Ave.
Albany, NY 12203 (518) 438-4929

BUFFALO: Dent Neurological Institute
Millard Fillmore Hospital
3 Gate Circle
Buffalo, NY 14209 (716) 873-2988

MANHATTAN: 32 W. Broadway
New York, NY 10004 (212) 736-3670 or (201) 224-0388

125 W. 76 St.
New York, NY 10023 (212) 873-0216

NASSAU AND
SUFFOLK COUNTIES: 579 Monroe St.
Cedarhurst, NY 11516 (516) 569-2310

ROCHESTER: 24 Harvard St.
Rochester, NY 14607 (716) 442-3820
(716) 473-1634

WESTCHESTER: 785 Mamaroneck
White Plains, NY 10605 (914) 428-1919

## NORTH CAROLINA

DURHAM: Duke Family Support Network
Room 153, Civitan Bldg.
Duke University Medical Center
Durham, NC 27710 (919) 684-2328

## OHIO

ATHENS: 37 Pleasant View Dr.
Athens, OH 45701 (614) 592-2013
(614) 592-1913

CANTON: 1509 Howensting Dr. S.E.
East Sparta, OH 44626 (216) 484-5878

CINCINNATI: 8995 Tripoli Dr.
Cincinnati, OH 45239 (513) 729-3271

CLEVELAND: 1801 Chestnut Hills Dr.
Cleveland, OH 44106 (216) 721-8457

COLUMBUS: Martin Janis Senior Center
600 East 11 Ave.
Columbus, OH 43211 (614) 299-2327

DAYTON 157 Shenandoah Trail
West Carrollton, OH 45449 (513) 435-0151

YOUNGSTOWN: 344 S. Broad St.
Canfield, OH 44406 (216) 533-7234

## OKLAHOMA

OAKLAHOMA CITY: 1613 Andover Ct.,
Oaklahoma City, OK 73120
(405) 843-4680

## OREGON

COLUMBIA-WILLAMETTE: (located in the Portland area)
Neurological Sciences Center
Good Samaritan Hospital
1015 NW 22 Ave.
Portland, OR 97210
(503) 232-0306

## PENNSYLVANIA

PITTSBURGH: 1201 Arrott Building
401 Wood St. (412) 469-1567
Pittsburgh, PA 15222 (412) 355-5248

PHILADELPHIA: 821 Clifford Ave. (215) 649-3198
Ardmore, PA 19003 (215) 485-4528
2424 Easton
Apt. D-3
Willow Grove, PA 19090 (215) 441-4614

## RHODE ISLAND

PROVIDENCE: Gerontology Center
Rhode Island College
600 Mt. Pleasant Ave.
Providence, RI 02908 (401) 456-8276

## TENNESSEE

MEMPHIS: 4060 Southlawn Ave.
Memphis, TN 38111 (901) 744-1165

## TEXAS

AMARILLO: Route 6, Box 760
Amarillo, TX 79106 (806) 381-1010

DALLAS: 11216 Dumbarton (214) 948-7973
Dallas, TX 75228 (214) 270-9604

EL PASO: 6545 Fiesta Dr.
El Paso, TX 79912 (915) 581-4926

FORT WORTH: 2925 Conejos Dr.
Fort Worth, TX 76116 (817) 244-1085

HOUSTON: 8101 Amelia #304 (713) 869-5546
Houston, TX 77055 (713) 465-9505

## UTAH

OGDEN: 3243 Van Buren
Ogden, UT 84403 (801) 399-9422

## VIRGINIA

HAMPTON ROADS: Comprehensive Mental Health Service
Pembroke Three, Suite 109
Virginia Beach, VA 23462
(804) 490-0583

NORTHERN VIRGINIA: P.O. Box 2715
Springfield, VA 22152
(703) 273-5453

RICHMOND: P.O. Box 3185
Richmond,VA 23235 (804) 794-9723
1163 Southham Dr.
Richmond, VA 23235 (804) 320-3365

SALEM/ROANOKE: VA Medical Center (703) 982-2463
Salem, VA 24153 Ext. 2477

## WISCONSIN

MILWAUKEE: Wisconsin Regional Geriatric Center
Family Hospital
2711 W. Wells St. (414) 933-6769
Milwaukee, WI 53208 (414) 547-6406

## ENGLAND

## ALZHEIMER'S DISEASE SOCIETY

AVON: 65 Belmont Road,
Bristol 6 0272 40570

21 Caledonian Place,
Clifton, Bristol 0273 39053

BEDS: 9 Sherringham Close,
Warren Hill, Luton 0782 58263

BERKS: 5 The Mews,
Hamilton Road, Reading 0734 669475

BOURNEMOUTH: 169 Malvern Road,
Moordown, Bournemouth 0202 526684

BUCKS: 33A Poppy Road,
Princes Risborough 08444 5098

CAMBS: Dyke Moor Farm,
Dykemoore N, Primrose Hill,
NR. March, Doddington 0354 740381

CHICHESTER: 21 Church Street, Richards Road,
Westgate 024 368 2441

CORNWALL: St. Lawrence Hospital,
Bodmin 0208 3281

DORSET: (Birdport Area) SS Department,
The Grove, Ray Lane

ESSEX: 26 Daking Avenue,
Boxford 0787 210192

GLOS: Rosegarth, Soudley,
Cinderford 0594 23528

GRIMSBY, HULL & LINCOLN: 12 Roundway, Grimsby, S.,
Humberside 0472 78187

HANTS: 106 Rollestone Road,
Fawley 0703 891669

29 Greenway Close,
Pennington, Lymington 0590 75911

HERTS: 9 Sherringham Close,
Warren Hill, Luton 0782 582632

ISLE OF WIGHT: 31 Upton Road,
Ryde 0983 62026

KENT: (Bromley Area) 50 Kelsey Lane,
Beckenham 01 650 7787

LEEDS: 29 Henley View,
Bramley 5032 553534

LEICESTER: 7 Chalvington Close,
Leicester 0533 41 2154

LEICESTERSHIRE and NOTT: 11 Belvoir Way,
Shepshed, Loughborough
05095 4194

LONDON: 1A Winterwell Road,
London SW2 01 737 2641

MANCHESTER: 18 Malvern Close,
Prestwich 061 773 9333

MERSEYSIDE: 21 Halkirk Road,
Hallerton, Liverpool 051 427 6418

OXFORD: 29 St. Andrew's Road,
Headington, Oxford 0865 62887

SURREY: Darren House,
Woodland Way, Weybridge 97 52481

44 Redstone Park,
Redhill 91 62608

9 Simon's Court,
Lovelace Road, Surbiton 01 399 3883

11 Pewley Hill,
Guildford 0483 67896

SUFFOLK: 282 Tuddenham Road,
Ipswich 0473 213554

SHEFFIELD: 38 Dobcroft Road,
Sheffield 0742 36387

SCOTLAND GLASGOW
and EDINBURGH: Andrew Duncan Clinic,
Edinburgh 031 447 2011

SUSSEX HOVE and BRIGHTON: 62 Farm Court Road,
Hove 0273 723489

TYNE and WEAR: 19 Cyprus Gardens,
Low Fell, Gateshead 0632 871131

WEST MIDLANDS: 108 Cecily Road,
Coventry 0203 503346

WARWICK HEREFORD
and WORCS.: 4 Ragley Crescent, Broom Park,
Bromsgrove, Worcs 0527 33202

W. YORKS: 69 Kirkpath, Shipley

WILTS: 2A Junction Road,
Bradford-on-Avon 02216 2112

**COMMITTEE TO COMBAT HUNTINGTON'S DISEASE**
**NATIONAL CCHD HEADQUARTERS**

250 W. 57 St.
Suite 2016
New York, NY 10107
(212) 757-0443

Chapters as of October 1982

**ARIZONA**

PHOENIX: 7506 N. 22 Place
Phoenix, AZ 85020 (602) 997-2776

**CALIFORNIA**

LOS ANGELES: 429 N. Maple Dr. (213) 825-0200 (O)
Beverly Hills, CA 90210 (213) 274-2776 (H)

NORTHERN CALIFORNIA: c/o Chapter President
(415) 254-6280

SAN DIEGO COUNTY: 1294 Clarke Dr.
El Cajon, CA 92021 (714) 447-7445

## COLORADO

ROCKY MOUNTAIN: 9282 E. Eastman Place
Denver, CO 80231 (303) 751-2249

P.O. Box 146
Aurora, CO 80040

## CONNECTICUT

STAMFORD: 74 Bangall Rd.
Stamford, CT 06903 (203) 329-8615

## DISTRICT OF COLUMBIA

WASHINGTON METRO AREA: (703) 978-8752

## GEORGIA

DECATUR: P.O. Box 245
Decatur, GA 30031 (404) 979-2096

## ILLINOIS

CHICAGO: 5116 N. Cicero
Chicago, IL 60630 (312) 282-3726

## INDIANA

MADISON: Huntington's Office
Rehabilitation Therapy
A.T. Building
Madison State Hospital
Madison, IN 47250 (812) 265-7408

## IOWA

DES MOINES: P.O. Box 137
Des Moines, IA 50301

**KANSAS**

WICHITA: P.O. Box 2413
Wichita, KS 67201

2721 Boulevard Plaza
Wichita, KS 67211 (316) 684-0593

**MARYLAND**

ELLICOTT CITY: P.O. Box 14
Ellicott City, MD 21043 (301) 730-9326

**MASSACHUSETTS**

BOSTON: Boston University Medical Center
80 East Concord St.
Boston, MA 02118 (617) 247-5049

**MICHIGAN**

MADISON HEIGHTS: Box 111
Madison Heights, MI 48071
(313) 465-7550

**MINNESOTA**

NORTH CENTRAL: Dight Institute for Human Genetics
University of Minnesota
400 Church St. S.E.
Minneapolis, MN 55455 (612) 373-3797

**MISSOURI**

ST. LOUIS: 3 Valley View Place
St. Louis, MO 63124 (314) 991-1192

**NEW YORK**

ROCHESTER: 390 Peart Ave.
Rochester, NY 14622 (716) 467-2425

## OHIO

COLUMBUS/MT. VERNON—
NORTHEAST: 14805 Detroit Ave.
Suite 210
Lakewood, OH 44107 (216) 221-8741

## OKLAHOMA

OKLAHOMA CITY: Department of Pediatrics
University of Oklahoma Health Science Center
P.O. Box 26901
Oklahoma City, OK 73190
(405) 271-2227

## OREGON

PORTLAND: 5000 N. Willamette Blvd.
Portland, OR 97203 (503) 283-7111

## PENNSYLVANIA

DELAWARE VALLEY: Windsor Apartments
17 & Benjamin Franklin Parkway
Suite 2308
Philadelphia, PA 19102
(215) 569-0536

## SOUTH CAROLINA

COLUMBIA: P.O. Box 21875
Columbia, SC 29221

## SOUTH DAKOTA

SIOUX VALLEY: P.O. Box 1031
Sioux Falls, SD 57101 (605) 446-3555

## WASHINGTON

PUGET SOUND: P.O. Box 88521
Seattle, WA 98188 (206) 543-8530

## WISCONSIN

JANESVILLE: P.O. Box 1073
Janesville, WI 53547 (608) 754-8261

BRANCHES OF CCHD

| | |
|---|---|
| CALIFORNIA | Sunnymead |
| | Sacramento |
| ILLINOIS | Rockford |
| INDIANA | Carmel |
| | Hammond |
| IOWA | Davenport |
| KANSAS | Topeka |
| PENNSYLVANIA | Beaver |
| | Harrisburg |

FRIENDS OF CCHD

| | |
|---|---|
| KENTUCKY | Lexington |
| OHIO | Toledo |
| TEXAS | San Antonio |
| WEST VIRGINIA | Parkersburg |

SELF-HELP GROUPS

| | |
|---|---|
| FLORIDA | Jacksonville |
| IOWA | Cedar Rapids |
| NEBRASKA | Lincoln |
| NEW YORK | Port Crane |
| OHIO | Cincinnati |

# APPENDIX C

# METHODS OF ESTIMATING RISKS FOR DISEASE WITH KNOWN FAMILIAL RISKS

The remaining risk at age $x$, given the total risk over a lifetime, and the distribution of ages at onset, can be estimated from the following equation:

$$\text{Risk at age } x$$

$$= \frac{\text{Risk at birth (1 − proportion of cases which become ill by age } x)}{1 - \text{risk at birth} \times \text{proportion of cases which become ill by age } x}$$

For example, following the Huntington's disease problem described in the text of Chapter 5 and illustrated in Figure 5.1, we know that 50 percent of the children of a parent with Huntington's disease will themselves develop the disease. We also know that half of those who do develop the disease will do so by age forty-six (approximately). Fitting those numbers into the equation set out above yields the following risk for the child of a Huntington's parent alive and well at age forty-six:

$$\text{Risk remaining at age 46} = \frac{0.5\ (1 - 0.5)}{1 - 0.5 \times 0.5} = \frac{0.25}{0.75} = \frac{1}{3} = 0.33$$

The risk at birth (or the lifetime risk or the morbid risk) is the risk or probability that a given disease will develop over the lifetime of a person newly born. It is known in some cases from genetic theory; for example, it is 0.5 for Huntington's disease for the child of a parent affected with the disease. For other diseases the risk is *empirical;* that is, it is estimated on the basis of accumulated experience with the illness. This is the case with both DAT and Pick's. The empirical risks for those diseases are given in the tables included in this section.

For an example of the use of this empirical information, suppose that we want to estimate the remaining risk of a forty-five-year-old person whose parent has Pick's disease. We see from Table C–3 (this appendix) that the morbid risk for Pick's disease for a first-degree relative of a victim of the disease is 25 percent. From the entries in the table, we may estimate by extrapolation that by age forty-five, 13 percent of those who will develop the disease will have already done so. Then using the equation given earlier, the remaining risk for the son or daughter of an affected person who is well at age forty-five may be estimated as:

$$\text{Risk remaining at age 45} = \frac{0.25\ (1 - 0.13)}{1 - 0.25 \times 0.13} = 0.22$$

To perform the same arithmetic for DAT, use the family types depicted in Figure 5.2 and the estimates given in Figures 5.3 and 5.4. If a perfect match for family type cannot be found, use the closest one.

One more realistic example: We want to know the risk for the daughter of a man with Huntington's chorea and for her son. The daughter will be twenty-eight-years old in one month and she has no sign of Huntington's disease. Her son is eight years and one month old. In Table C–1, we see that the twenty-eight-year-old daughter has outlived between 5.4 percent (the proportion affected by age twenty-five) and 13 percent (the proportion affected by age thirty) of the total risk of 50 percent. Let us estimate that the daughter has lived through 10 percent of her risk—that estimate will be quite close enough for practical purposes. For the rest of her life her remaining risk can be estimated as:

$$\text{Risk remaining at age 27 years, 11 months} = \frac{0.5\ (1 - 0.1)}{1 - 0.5 \times 0.1} = 0.47$$

The risk to her son will be one-half of her risk—or 0.235. This is because the son has one-half of the genes possessed by his mother and, therefore, one-half of her chance for having the gene associated with the disease.

Variations of the problems described in this appendix are representative of those that arise in real-life situations. However, there are many restrictions and caveats which may be relevant in a specific case. If there is the slightest doubt about the applicability of the formulas or the estimated risks, consult a genetic counselor. Most major medical centers will be able to make appropriate referrals to such a person. The stakes may be too high to warrant any doubts about the accuracy of the results you may obtain. However, working through specific problems using the above formulas will, at worst, be most valuable preparation for a visit to a counselor.

***Table C–1 Age at Onset of Huntington's Disease (Lifetime risk for first-degree relative = 0.5)***

| AGE INTERVAL | PERCENT WITH ONSET IN INTERVAL | CUMULATIVE PERCENTAGE |
|---|---|---|
| –10 | 0.1 | 0.1 |
| 11–15 | 0.7 | 0.8 |
| 16–20 | 1.4 | 2.2 |
| 21–25 | 3.2 | 5.4 |
| 26–30 | 7.6 | 13.0 |
| 31–35 | 8.9 | 21.9 |
| 36–40 | 13.4 | 35.3 |
| 41–45 | 16.4 | 51.7 |
| 46–50 | 19.8 | 71.5 |
| 51–55 | 14.0 | 85.5 |
| 56–60 | 9.6 | 95.1 |
| 61–65 | 3.5 | 98.6 |
| 66–70 | 1.1 | 99.7 |
| 71– | 0.3 | 100.0 |

*Table C–2 Age at Onset for Dementia of the Alzheimer Type*

| AGE INTERVAL | PERCENT WITH ONSET IN INTERVAL | CUMULATIVE PERCENTAGE |
|---|---|---|
| –44 | 2 | 2 |
| 45–49 | 3 | 5 |
| 50–54 | 5 | 10 |
| 55–59 | 7 | 17 |
| 60–64 | 14 | 31 |
| 65–69 | 19 | 50 |
| 70–74 | 17 | 67 |
| 75–79 | 16 | 83 |
| 80–84 | 12 | 95 |
| 85– | 5 | 100 |

(Lifetime empirical risk for a first-degree relative estimated as 0.30. But risks are age-specific and vary with family type. If possible, use risks estimated from Figures 5.2 and 5.3 in Chapter 5.)

*Table C–3 Age at Onset for Pick's Disease (Lifetime empirical risk to first-degree relatives estimated at 0.25)*

| AGE INTERVAL | PERCENT FALLING ILL | CUMULATIVE PERCENTAGE |
|---|---|---|
| –39 | 7 | 7 |
| 40–49 | 13 | 20 |
| 50–59 | 38 | 58 |
| 60–69 | 28 | 86 |
| 70– | 14 | 100 |

# APPENDIX D

# WHERE TO WRITE FOR VITAL RECORDS

**ALABAMA**

| | | |
|---|---|---|
| Birth or death | \$5.00 | Bureau of Vital Statistics<br>State Department of<br>Public Health<br>Montgomery, AL 36130 |

*Remarks:* State office has had records since January 1908. Additional copies at same time are \$2.00 each. Fee for special searches is \$5.00 per hour.

**ALASKA**

| | | |
|---|---|---|
| Birth or death | \$3.00 | Department of Health and<br>Social Services<br>Bureau of Vital Statistics<br>Pouch H-02G<br>Juneau, AK 99811 |

*Remarks:* State office has had records since 1913.

## AMERICAN SAMOA

| | | |
|---|---|---|
| Birth or death | $1.00 | Registrar of Vital Statistics<br>Vital Statistics Section<br>Government of American Samoa<br>Pago Pago, AS 96799 |

*Remarks:* Registrar has had records since 1900.

## ARIZONA

| | | |
|---|---|---|
| Birth or death | $3.00 | Vital Records Section<br>Arizona Department of Health Services<br>P.O. Box 3887<br>Phoenix, AZ 85030 |

*Remarks:* State office has had records since July 1909 and abstracts of records filed in counties before then.

## ARKANSAS

| | | |
|---|---|---|
| Birth<br>Death | $2.00<br>$3.00 | Division of Vital Records<br>Arkansas Department of Health<br>4815 West Markham St.<br>Little Rock, AR 72201 |

*Remarks:* State office has had records since February 1914 and has some original Little Rock and Fort Smith records from 1881.

## CALIFORNIA

| | | |
|---|---|---|
| Birth or death | $3.00 | Vital Statistics Branch<br>Department of Health Services<br>410 N Street<br>Sacramento, CA 95814 |

*Remarks:* State office has had records since July 1905. For earlier records, write to County Recorder in county where event occurred.

## CANAL ZONE

| | | |
|---|---|---|
| Birth or death | $2.00 | Panama Canal Commission<br>Vital Statistics Clerk<br>APO Miami 34011 |

*Remarks:* Records available from May 1904 to September 1979.

## COLORADO

| | | |
|---|---|---|
| Birth or death | $2.00 | Vital Records Section<br>Colorado Department of Health<br>4210 East 11 Avenue<br>Denver, CO 80220 |

*Remarks:* State office has had death records since 1900 and birth records since 1910. State office also has birth records for some counties for years before 1910.

## CONNECTICUT

| | | |
|---|---|---|
| Birth or death | $3.00 | Department of Health Services<br>Vital Records Section<br>Division of Health Statistics<br>79 Elm St.<br>Hartford, CT 06115 |
| Short form | $2.00 | |

*Remarks:* State office has had records since July 1897. For earlier records, write to Registrar of Vital Statistics in town or city where event occurred.

## DELAWARE

| | | |
|---|---|---|
| Birth or death | $2.50 | Bureau of Vital Statistics<br>Division of Public Health<br>Department of Health and |

| | | |
|---|---|---|
| | | Social Services<br>State Health Building<br>Dover, DE 19901 |

*Remarks:* State office has records for 1861 to 1863 and since 1881 but no records for 1864 to 1880.

## DISTRICT OF COLUMBIA

| | | |
|---|---|---|
| Birth or death | $3.00 | Vital Records Branch<br>615 Pennsylvania Ave. N.W.<br>Washington, DC 20004 |

*Remarks:* Office has had death records since 1855 and birth records since 1871, but no death records were filed during the Civil War.

## FLORIDA

| | | |
|---|---|---|
| Birth or death | $2.00 | Department of Health and Rehabilitative Services<br>Office of Vital Statistics<br>P.O. Box 210<br>Jacksonville, FL 32231 |

*Remarks:* State office has had some birth records since April 1865 and some death records since August 1877. The majority of records date from January 1917. If the exact date is unknown, the fee is $2.00 for the first year searched and $1.00 for each additional year up to a maximum of $25.00. Fee includes one copy of record if found.

## GEORGIA

| | | |
|---|---|---|
| Birth or death | $3.00 | Georgia Department of Human Resources<br>Vital Records Unit<br>Room 217-H<br>47 Trinity Ave. S.W.<br>Atlanta, GA 30334 |

*Remarks:* State office has had records since January 1919. For earlier records in Atlanta or Savannah, write to County Health

Department in county where event occurred. Additional copies of same record ordered at same time are $1.00 each.

**GUAM**

| | | |
|---|---|---|
| Birth or death | $2.00 | Office of Vital Statistics<br>Department of Public Health and Social Services<br>Government of Guam<br>P.O. Box 2816<br>Agana, GU, M.I. 96910 |

*Remarks:* Office has had records since October 26, 1901.

**HAWAII**

| | | |
|---|---|---|
| Birth or death | $2.00 | Research and Statistics Office<br>State Department of Health<br>P.O. Box 3378<br>Honolulu, HI 96801 |

*Remarks:* State office has had records since 1853.

**IDAHO**

| | | |
|---|---|---|
| Birth or death | $4.00 | Bureau of Vital Statistics, Standards, and Local Health Services<br>State Department of Health and Welfare<br>Statehouse<br>Boise, ID 83720 |

*Remarks:* State office has had records since 1911. For records from 1907 to 1911, write to County Recorder in county where event occurred.

**ILLINOIS**

| | | |
|---|---|---|
| Birth or death | $3.00 | Office of Vital Records<br>State Department of Public Health |

535 West Jefferson St.
Springfield, IL 62761

*Remarks:* State office has had records since January 1916. For earlier records and for copies of state records since January 1916, write to County Clerk in county where event occurred. $3.00 fee is for search of files and one copy of record if found. Additional copies of same record ordered at same time are $2.00 each.

**INDIANA**

| | | |
|---|---|---|
| Birth or death | $4.00 | Division of Vital Records<br>State Board of Health<br>1330 West Michigan St.<br>P.O. Box 1964<br>Indianapolis, IN 46206 |

*Remarks:* State office has had birth records since October 1907 and death records since 1900. Additional copies of same record ordered at same time are $1.00 each. For earlier records, write to Health Officer in city or county where event occurred.

**IOWA**

| | | |
|---|---|---|
| Birth or death | $4.00 | Iowa State Department of Health<br>Vital Records Section<br>Lucas State Office Building<br>Des Moines, IA 50319 |

*Remarks:* State office has had records since July 1880.

**KANSAS**

| | | |
|---|---|---|
| Birth or death | $3.00 | Bureau of Registration and Health Statistics<br>Kansas State Department of Health and Environment<br>6700 South Topeka Ave.<br>Topeka, KS 66620 |

*Remarks:* State office has had records since July 1911. For earlier records, write to County Clerk in county where event occurred. Additional copies of same record ordered at same time are $2.00 each.

## KENTUCKY

| | | |
|---|---|---|
| Birth or death | $4.00 | Office of Vital Statistics<br>Department of Human Resources<br>275 East Main St.<br>Frankfort, KY 40621 |

*Remarks:* State office has had records since January 1911 and some records for the cities of Louisville, Lexington, Covington, and Newport before then.

## LOUISIANA

| | | |
|---|---|---|
| Birth or death<br>Short form | $3.00<br>$2.00 | Division of Vital Records<br>Office of Health Services and Environmental Quality<br>P.O. Box 60630<br>New Orleans, LA 70160 |

*Remarks:* State office has had records since July 1914. Birth records for city of New Orleans are available from 1790, and death records from 1803.

## MAINE

| | | |
|---|---|---|
| Birth or death | $2.00 | Office of Vital Records<br>Human Services Building<br>Station II<br>Statehouse<br>Augusta, ME 04333 |

*Remarks:* State office has had records since 1892. For earlier records, write to the municipality where event occurred.

## MARYLAND

| | | |
|---|---|---|
| Birth or death | \$2.00 | Division of Vital Records<br>State Department of Health and Mental Hygiene<br>State Office Building<br>P.O. Box 13146<br>201 West Preston St.<br>Baltimore, MD 21203 |

*Remarks:* State office has had records since August 1898. Records for city of Baltimore are available from January 1875.

## MASSACHUSETTS

| | | |
|---|---|---|
| Birth or death | \$3.00 | Registry of Vital Records and Statistics<br>Room 105, McCormack Building<br>1 Ashburton Place<br>Boston, MA 02108 |

*Remarks:* State office has had records, except for Boston, since 1841. For earlier records, write to the City or Town Clerk in place where event occurred. Earliest records available in the Boston office are for 1848.

## MICHIGAN

| | | |
|---|---|---|
| Birth or death | \$10.00 | Office of Vital and Health Statistics<br>Michigan Department of Public Health<br>3500 North Logan St.<br>Lansing, MI 48914 |

*Remarks:* State office has had records since 1867. Copies of records since 1867 may also be obtained from County Clerk in county where event occurred. Detroit records may be obtained from the City Health Department for births occurring since 1893 and for deaths since 1897.

## MINNESOTA

| | | |
|---|---|---|
| Birth or death | $5.00 | Minnesota Department of Health<br>Section of Vital Statistics<br>717 Delaware St. S.E.<br>Minneapolis, MN 55440 |

*Remarks:* State office has had records since January 1908. Copies of earlier records may be obtained from Clerk of District Court in county where event occurred or from the Minneapolis or St. Paul City Health Department if the event occurred in either city.

## MISSISSIPPI

| | | |
|---|---|---|
| Birth | $10.00 | Vital Records |
| Short form | $ 5.00 | State Board of Health |
| Death | $ 5.00 | P.O. Box 1700 |
| | | Jackson, MS 39205 |

*Remarks:* State office has had records since 1912. Full copies of birth certificates obtained within one year after the event are $5.00. Additional copies of same record ordered at same time are $1.00 each.

## MISSOURI

| | | |
|---|---|---|
| Birth or death | $4.00 | Division of Health<br>Bureau of Vital Records<br>State Department of Health and Welfare<br>Jefferson City, MO 65101 |

*Remarks:* State office has had records since January 1910. If event occurred in St. Louis (city), St. Louis County, or Kansas City before 1910, write to the City or County Health Department. Copies of these records are $3.00 each in St. Louis, city or county. In Kansas City, $6.00 for first copy and $3.00 for each additional copy ordered at same time.

## MONTANA

| | | |
|---|---|---|
| Birth or death | $3.00 | Bureau of Records and Statistics<br>State Department of Health and Environmental Sciences<br>Helena, MT 59601 |

*Remarks:* State office has had records since late 1907.

## NEBRASKA

| | | |
|---|---|---|
| Birth or death | $5.00 | Bureau of Vital Statistics<br>State Department of Health<br>301 Centennial Mall South<br>P.O. Box 95007<br>Lincoln, NE 68509 |

*Remarks:* State office has had records since late 1904. If birth occurred before then, write the state office for information.

## NEVADA

| | | |
|---|---|---|
| Birth or death | $4.00 | Division of Health and Vital Statistics<br>Capitol Complex<br>Carson City, NV 89710 |

*Remarks:* State office has had records since July 1911. For earlier records, write to County Recorder in county where event occurred. Additional copies of death records ordered at the same time are $4.00 for second and third copies, $3.00 each for the next three copies, and $2.00 each for any additional copies.

## NEW HAMPSHIRE

| | | |
|---|---|---|
| Birth or death | $3.00 | Bureau of Vital Records<br>Health and Welfare Building |

Hazen Drive
Concord, NH 03301

*Remarks:* State office has had some records since 1640. Copies of records may be obtained from state office or from City or Town Clerk in place where event occurred.

**NEW JERSEY**

| | | |
|---|---|---|
| Birth or death | $2.00 | State Department of Health<br>Bureau of Vital Statistics<br>CN 360<br>Trenton, NJ 08625 |

*Remarks:* State office has had records since June 1878. Additional copies of same record ordered at same time are $1.00 each. If the exact date is unknown, fee is an additional $0.50 per year searched. Records from May 1848 to May 1878 are available from Archives and History Bureau, State Library Division, State Department of Education, Trenton, NJ 08625.

**NEW MEXICO**

| | | |
|---|---|---|
| Birth or death | $4.00 | Vital Statistics Bureau<br>New Mexico Health Services Division<br>P.O. Box 968<br>Santa Fe, NM 87503 |

*Remarks:* State office has had records since 1920 and delayed records since 1880.

**NEW YORK (except New York City)**

| | | |
|---|---|---|
| Birth or death | $5.00 | Bureau of Vital Records<br>State Department of Health<br>Empire State Plaza<br>Tower Building<br>Albany, NY 12237 |

*Remarks:* State office has had records since 1880. For records before 1914 in Albany, Buffalo, and Yonkers or before 1880 in any other city, write to Registrar of Vital Statistics in city where event occurred. For the rest of the state, except New York City, write to state office.

## NEW YORK CITY

| | | |
|---|---|---|
| Birth or death | $4.00 | Bureau of Vital Records<br>Department of Health of New York City<br>125 Worth St.<br>New York, NY 10013 |

*Remarks:* Office has had birth records since 1898 and death records since 1920. For Old City of New York (Manhattan and part of the Bronx) birth records for 1865–1897 and death records for 1865–1919, write to Municipal Archives and Records Retention, 52 Chambers St., New York, NY 10038.

## NORTH CAROLINA

| | | |
|---|---|---|
| Birth or death | $3.00 | Department of Human Resources<br>Division of Health Services<br>Vital Records Branch<br>P.O. Box 2091<br>Raleigh, NC 27602 |

*Remarks:* State office has had birth records since October 1913 and death records since January 1, 1930. Death records from 1913 through 1929 are available from Archives and Records Section, State Records Center, 215 North Blount St., Raleigh, NC 27602.

## NORTH DAKOTA

| | | |
|---|---|---|
| Birth or death | $2.00 | Division of Vital Records<br>State Department of Health<br>Office of Statistical Services<br>Bismarck, ND 58505 |

*Remarks:* State office has had some records since July 1893. Years from 1894 to 1920 are incomplete.

## OHIO

| | | |
|---|---|---|
| Birth or death | $3.00 | Division of Vital Statistics<br>Ohio Department of Health<br>G-20 Ohio Departments Building<br>65 South Front St.<br>Columbus, OH 43215 |

*Remarks:* State office has had records since December 20, 1908. For earlier records, write to Probate Court in county where event occurred.

## OKLAHOMA

| | | |
|---|---|---|
| Birth or death | $2.00 | Vital Records Section<br>State Department of Health<br>Northeast 10 St. & Stonewall<br>P.O. Box 53551<br>Oklahoma City, OK 73152 |

*Remarks:* State office has had records since October 1908.

## OREGON

| | | |
|---|---|---|
| Birth or death | $5.00 | Oregon State Health Division<br>Vital Statistics Section<br>P.O. Box 116<br>Portland, OR 97207 |

*Remarks:* State office has had records since January 1903. Some earlier records for the city of Portland since approximately 1880 are available from the Oregon State Archives, 1005 Broadway N.E., Salem, OR 97310.

## PENNSYLVANIA

| | | |
|---|---|---|
| Birth | $4.00 | Division of Vital Statistics<br>State Department of Health<br>Central Building<br>101 South Mercer St.<br>P.O. Box 1528<br>New Castle, PA 16103 |
| Short form | $5.00 | |
| Death | $3.00 | |

*Remarks:* State office has had records since January 1906. For earlier records, write to Register of Wills, Orphans Court, in county seat where event occurred. Persons born in Pittsburgh from 1870 to 1905 or in Allegheny City, now part of Pittsburgh, from 1882 to 1905 should write to Office of Biostatistics, Pittsburgh Health Department, City-County Building, Pittsburgh, PA 15219. For events occurring in city of Philadelphia from 1860 to 1915, write to Vital Statistics, Philadelphia Department of Public Health, City Hall Annex, Philadelphia, PA 19107.

## PUERTO RICO

| | | |
|---|---|---|
| Birth or death | $0.50 | Division of Demographic Registry and Vital Statistics<br>Department of Health<br>San Juan, PR 00908 |

*Remarks:* Central office has had records since July 22, 1931. Copies of earlier records may be obtained by writing to local Registrar (Registrador Demografico) in municipality where event occurred or by writing to central office for information.

## RHODE ISLAND

| | | |
|---|---|---|
| Birth or death | $4.00 | Division of Vital Statistics<br>State Department of Health<br>Room 101, Cannon Building<br>75 Davis St.<br>Providence, RI 02908 |

*Remarks:* State office has had records since 1853. For earlier records, write to Town Clerk in town where event occurred. Additional copies of the same record ordered at the same time are $2.00 each.

## SOUTH CAROLINA

| | | |
|---|---|---|
| Birth or death | $3.00 | Office of Vital Records and Public Health Statistics<br>S.C. Department of Health and Environmental Control<br>2600 Bull St.<br>Columbia, SC 29201 |

*Remarks:* State office has had records since January 1915. City of Charleston births from 1877 and deaths from 1821 are on file at Charleston County Health Department. Ledger entries of Florence City births and deaths from 1895 to 1914 are on file at Florence County Health Department. Ledger entries of Newberry City births and deaths from late 1800s are on file at Newberry County Health Department. These are the only early records obtainable.

## SOUTH DAKOTA

| | | |
|---|---|---|
| Birth or death | $3.00 | State Department of Health<br>Health Statistics Program<br>Joe Foss Office Building<br>Pierre, SD 57501 |

*Remarks:* State office has had records since July 1905 and access to other records for some events that occurred before then. Additional copies requested at the same time are $1.00 each.

## TENNESSEE

| | | |
|---|---|---|
| Birth | $6.00 | Division of Vital Records |
| Death | $4.00 | State Department of Public Health |

| | | |
|---|---|---|
| | | Cordell Hull Building<br>Nashville, TN 37219 |

*Remarks:* State office has had birth records for entire state since January 1914, for Nashville since June 1881, for Knoxville since July 1881, and for Chattanooga since January 1882. State office has had death records for entire state since January 1914, for Nashville since July 1874, for Knoxville since July 1887, and for Chattanooga since March 1872. Birth and death enumeration records by school district are available for July 1908 through June 1912. For Memphis birth records from April 1874 through December 1887 and November 1898 through December 1913, and for Memphis death records from May 1848 through December 1913, write to Memphis-Shelby County Health Department, Division of Vital Records, Memphis, TN 38105.

## TEXAS

| | | |
|---|---|---|
| Birth or death | \$5.00 | Bureau of Vital Statistics<br>Texas Department of Health<br>1100 West 49 St.<br>Austin, TX 78756 |

*Remarks:* State office has had records since 1903. Additional copies of same death record ordered at same time are \$2.00 each.

## TRUST TERRITORY OF THE PACIFIC ISLANDS

| | | |
|---|---|---|
| Birth or death | \$0.25 plus \$0.10 per 100 words | Director of Medical Services<br>Department of Medical Services<br>Saipan, Mariana Islands 96950 |

*Remarks:* Clerks of Court in district where event occurred have had records since November 1952. Beginning 1950, a few records have been filed with the Hawaii Bureau of Vital Statistics. If not sure of district in which event occurred, write

Director of Medical Services to have inquiry referred to the correct district.

## UTAH

| | | |
|---|---|---|
| Birth or death | $5.00 | Bureau of Health Statistics<br>Utah Department of Health<br>150 West North Temple<br>P.O. Box 2500<br>Salt Lake City, UT 84110 |

*Remarks:* State office has had records since 1905. If event occurred from 1890 to 1904 in Salt Lake City or Ogden, write to City Board of Health. For records elsewhere in the state from 1898 to 1904, write to County Clerk in county where event occurred.

## VERMONT

| | | |
|---|---|---|
| Birth or death | $3.00 | Vermont Department of Health<br>Vital Records Section<br>Box 70<br>115 Colchester Ave.<br>Burlington, VT 05401 |

*Remarks:* Town or City Clerk of town where birth or death occurred will also have records.

## VIRGINIA

| | | |
|---|---|---|
| Birth or death | $3.00 | Division of Vital Records and Health Statistics<br>State Department of Health<br>James Madison Building<br>P.O. Box 1000<br>Richmond, VA 23208 |

*Remarks:* State office has had records from January 1853 to December 1896 and since June 1912. For records between those dates, write to the Health Department in the city where the event occurred.

## VIRGIN ISLANDS (U.S.)

| | | |
|---|---|---|
| Birth or death | $2.00 | Registrar of Vital Statistics<br>Charles Harwood Memorial Hospital<br>St. Croix, VI 00820 |

*Remarks:* Registrar has had birth and death records on file since 1840 for St. Croix. For St. Thomas and St. John birth records on file since July 1906 and death records since January 1906, write to the Registrar of Vital Statistics, Charlott Amalie, St. Thomas, VI 00802.

## WASHINGTON

| | | |
|---|---|---|
| Birth or death | $3.00 | Vital Records<br>P.O. Box 9709, LB11<br>Olympia, WA 98504 |

*Remarks:* State office has had records since July 1907. For King, Pierce, and Spokane counties copies may also be obtained from county health departments. County Auditor of county of birth has registered births prior to July 1907.

## WEST VIRGINIA

| | | |
|---|---|---|
| Birth or death | $5.00 | Division of Vital Statistics<br>State Department of Health<br>State Office Building No. 3<br>Charleston, WV 25305 |

*Remarks:* State office has had records since January 1917. For earlier records, write to Clerk of County Court in county where event occurred.

## WISCONSIN

| | | |
|---|---|---|
| Birth or death | $4.00 | Bureau of Health Statistics<br>Wisconsin Division of Health<br>P.O. Box 309<br>Madison, WI 53701 |

*Remarks:* State office has scattered records earlier than 1857. Records before October 1907 are very incomplete. Additional copies of the same record ordered at the same time are $2.00 each.

## WYOMING

| | | |
|---|---|---|
| Birth or death | $2.00 | Vital Records Services<br>Division of Health and Medical Services<br>Hathaway Building<br>Cheyenne, WY 82002 |

*Remarks:* State office has had records since July 1909.

# INDEX